HARRY HOPKINS
AND THE NEW DEAL

HARRY HOPKINS
and the New Deal

by PAUL A. KURZMAN

Foreword by LOUIS W. KOENIG

R. E. BURDICK, Inc., *Publishers*
Fair Lawn, New Jersey

International Standard Book Number: 0-913638-07-2
Library of Congress Catalogue Card Number: 74-79260

Published by R.E. Burdick, Inc.,
12-01 12th Street, Fair Lawn, New Jersey 07410

Copyright ©1974 by Paul A. Kurzman

Published simultaneously in Canada
by the Book Center, Inc.,
1140 Beaulac Street, Montreal, Quebec H4R 1R8

Printed in the United States of America.

To
Margaret, Katherine *and* David

Contents

Foreword

MY INITIAL ENCOUNTER with the administrative world of Harry Hopkins occurred during my first employment, following graduate study, with the National Resources Planning Board. There I joined several former employees and associates of Hopkins' work relief organizations of the 30s. In our project at the Board, to plan for the longer-term human needs that government might meet, particularly for the period after World War II, with the reconversion from wartime to peacetime footing, I was impressed with several widely shared characteristics of the Hopkins people—with their imaginative, often creative, thinking about human problems and governmental responses, with their sturdy humanism, and with their bureaucratic *savoir-faire* for getting things done. In this definitive study by Paul Kurzman, it is apparent that these qualities pervaded Harry Hopkins' own contributions to the New Deal and assure his place as a central figure in the transformation of American social policy into a form that has a continuing relevance to the public problems of today.

Before assessing Hopkins' longer-term importance, it is necessary to consider first his contribution to the immediate world of the New Deal—the foundation on which that assessment must be built. In its beginnings, the New Deal confronted the paralysis of the Great Depression, with nearly one-fourth of the nation's work force unemployed, with the clear failure of the country's most experienced relief administrator, the outgoing President, Herbert Hoover, to overcome by traditional public policy and methods the gross malfunctions of the economy. Despite the confident tones of Franklin Roosevelt's inaugural address, the incoming President had no explicit program, no bagful of policies that he might draw upon to provide innovative programs to implement the generalities of his address. Policies and programs therefore had to be invented and contrived in a severely short time schedule and in the face of human need and discontent, which in some sectors of the country bordered on revolution.

Hopkins, whose frailty caused him to be likened to a matchstick or Ichabod Crane and masked an animation that was like a roaring furnace, was responsible for administering relief to the largest and most beset clientele of the New Deal, the vast army of the unemployed, most of whom had been gainfully employed all of their adult lives, only to be thrown into a state of joblessness for which neither they nor society was prepared. At this juncture in American history, the chief surcease for these people derived from state poor laws which designated that localities were to be responsible for caring for their needy. Characteristically, localities had few facilities except the almshouse, and prior conditions governing eligibility for receipt of benefits were degrading, typified by a mandatory pauper's oath and an atmosphere that suggested the unworthiness, if not the sinfulness, of the applicant. The other major source of assistance, private philanthropy, was little developed, genteel, and feeble in the face of the overwhelming needs of the Great Depression. Not even the beginnings of a serious, embracing program existed in the federal government.

Hopkins' task and contribution were to transform this

inadequate, incongruous, insensitive, and anachronistic response to the massive need into a nationwide program, designed to meet that need with equal concern for the unemployed in every state and, at the same time, to maintain human dignity. The genius of his contribution was his ability to accomplish this amidst the critical pressures of the New Deal. Hopkins' initial response, beginning in 1933, was as administrator of the Federal Emergency Relief Administration that provided hastily arranged work relief to the needy which evolved into special programs, such as those for farmers and teachers, and into many thousands of projects of public construction. Through FERA work relief, Hopkins made a giant stride in the revision of social welfare policy, moving it away from the historic standbys of the handout and the dole, and for the first time establishing the federal government as the principal source of response to the unemployed. FERA came to include other innovations—direct cash relief, auxiliary social services, and the use of the federal grant-in-aid to the states as a means of funneling federal assistance to the poor.

A second focus of Hopkins' redefinition of the character and thrust of social policy was the Civil Works Administration (CWA) designed by Hopkins and his staff for the looming crisis of the New Deal's first winter of 1933 and the heightened hardship that season would bring to the unemployed. In contrast to FERA, CWA was wholly a federal program, short-range—only for the winter months—and it was entirely a work program, designed and administered in ways even more conducive to maintaining or restoring the beneficiary's self-esteem. Participants in that work program were paid a cash wage at prevailing rates. The work offered included both white-collar and manual labor; and the projects were short-term, such as playground maintenance and road repair. In all, some 4,000,000 people were put to work, a larger force than those mobilized for major wars, and accomplished in far shorter time. By testimonials from far and wide, that grim winter of 1933 was diminished and surmounted by infusions of achievement and hope from CWA. Through CWA, Hopkins lifted work relief to a higher plateau of status and morale: CWA employed no means test; it accepted anyone who needed a job; it paid a cash wage instead of an allowance based on a family budget; and it fostered an identification with the job—a sense of working for the government—that at least began to approach its counterpart for the steel or automobile worker.

Hopkins' final major administrative enterprise in behalf of the unemployed was the Works Progress Administration (WPA), which he and his associates developed, sensing an opportunity in the sweeping Democratic victories in the 1934 elections for further innovation in .the social arena. Through WPA, Hopkins moved to replace relief with a permanent program of public works, under a formula by which the federal government would provide jobs whenever and for as long as they were needed, while returning to the states and localities the care of the unemployables. For the latter, traditional local responsibility was being reaffirmed; for the employables federal responsibility stemmed from the national character of their plight and the need for responses wholly different from the experiences and capabilities of the states. WPA was impressive and massive, with thousands upon thousands of projects, ranging from the construction of schools and post offices to the operation of a bankrupt municipal government.

Hopkins successfully injected into WPA the principle that the person receiving the assistance should do the kind of work for which his skills and training specially equip him. Consequently, WPA embraced projects for white-collar workers, for artists, actors and historians, for carpenters, masons and road builders, and myriad other occupations

and professions. It was a characteristic theory of Hopkins
that the dignity of an individual is best maintained when
his work matches his skills. Hopkins established his principle
as policy only after a courageous stand against a barrage of
jeers and jokes and political attacks for daring to suggest
that the skills of actors and artists are as worthy of governmental solicitude as those of accountants and engineers. In
the progression from FERA to CWA to WPA, Hopkins
moved the unemployed and the needy from a status of
semi-banishment, treated as objects or moral condescension,
to a new level far more in accord with the humanitarian
assumptions of a democratic society.

Hopkins' talent was not only conceptual, it was also practical. Both are essential for grand innovations of public
policy such as his. Hopkins' practicality applied to the internal politics of the executive branch, within the bureaucracy, in the orbit of the Presidency, and in the general
political system as well—in the politics of Congress, the
states, and the localities. Above all, he worked easily with
the complex, sometimes perfidious F.D.R. In the President's
esteem and graces, Hopkins was upwardly mobile, passing
every test, surmounting ever more difficult assignments,
moving into the circle of the President's advisers, and
emerging in the New Deal era eventually as the foremost
Presidential favorite. Hopkins' personal success with Roosevelt was indispensable to winning approval for the innovative design of WPA and its rapid implementation. Eventually Hopkins even dared entertain the notion of becoming
President himself, and Dr. Kurzman explores carefully
Hopkins' own attitudes, the question of Roosevelt's view
of Hopkins' possible candidacy, and the reactions of New
Deal associates. It is a facet of his life, we learn, that Hopkins was eager to have appear in the historic record.

To succeed with his relief projects, Hopkins had to

succeed in cabinet-level politics. His constant rival was the
crotchety, suspicious Secretary of the Interior, Harold L.
Ickes. Ickes administered a competing relief program,
scrambling with Hopkins for shares of the budgetary pie,
and for dominion over shifting program jurisdictions. It
was also a clash of personalities, a running feud between
the cautious, righteous Secretary and Hopkins, the fast-
actor, the knife-like penetrator of the bureaucratic defen-
sive armors of procedure and torpor, opinionated, never
jarred by hazard or obstacle. But Hopkins also excelled at
alliance politics at the cabinet level—his making of common
cause with fellow Secretaries and administrators to help win
a reluctant Roosevelt's acceptance of a comprehensive social
security system. This transpired after a long and careful
campaign against several F.D.R. attitudes toward social security, which initially found some of its features unpalatable.

In the bureaucratic world, Hopkins must hold something
of a record in the slender time he required to get a program started. In his first day on the job in Washington,
after notifying all the governors to set up state relief organizations, he dispensed some $5,000,000 in grants to seven
states. Hopkins, unlike other administrators, eschewed the
pace-slowing habits and formalities of bureaucratic procedures, the routines and dawdling clearances, the endless
paperwork. He sheared his way through obstructions, preferred oral communication to memoranda, shunned the
organization chart and convoluted tabulations of management specialists, and even though he was presiding master
of peacetime expenditures of unprecedented size, he par-
celled out the millions from offices that must rank among
the simplest and shabbiest in the long history of Washington
administrators. Against bureaucratic obstruction he was
fearless; he dared take on that most awesome of bureaucratic power centers, the Bureau of the Budget. Encoun-
tering adverse decisions there, he would rush to the White

House. Not only raw courage and natural competitiveness
impelled Hopkins to appeal; his flourishing personal relationship with Roosevelt time and again helped produce a
favorable decision.

Not surprisingly, given the nature of his policies, Hopkins faced politicians on Capitol Hill who, hoping to placate
tax-conscious constituents, derided Hopkins' programs and
his seemingly endless expenditures. It was a considerable
political accomplishment that Hopkins, nonetheless, could
move from one controversial, innovative program to another without suffering any serious setback. Behind Congressional tolerance was a satisfied public opinion that
perceived the gains that Hopkins' programs achieved in the
grimmest intervals of the Depression. By force of the
necessities of his programs, he excelled in the politics of
the federal system in evoking support and effective performance from state and local bureaucracies, and from
sundry governors and mayors. One of Hopkins' subtler
passages in federalism's politics stemmed from his insistence
upon decent relief policies for Negroes, a major step in
Roosevelt's general wooing of black people, leading to their
eventual detachment from their traditional Republican ties.
Simultaneously, Hopkins maintained especially constructive
relations with the Southern states. He never reproached or
preached to the South; but, aware of its special problems,
he was understanding and responsive to its economic and
social plight. In addition, several of Hopkins' top administrators were progressive Southerners, sources of informed
advice and confidence-building symbols for Hopkins' programs in their home terrain.

For Hopkins and his ground-breaking programs, politics
was also a world of limitations. He had to adjust his ideal
designs of social welfare to the tolerance of Congress and
public opinion, to the limits of appropriations and the
boundaries of laws. The theory of WPA could never be

carried out fully. There were always more people to employ
than there was money available to pay them. Congress and
the administration, restrained by tax-conscious public opinion, aimed to keep expenditures within reason. Admitting
some unemployed to participation in WPA while keeping
others out forced Hopkins to compromise with his welfare
ideals and to resort to means tests to determine eligibility,
evoking criticism from fellow social workers.

Politics imposed other limitations; but the wonder is that
Hopkins could extract so much political approval and support for programs that were highly vulnerable to administrative lapses and to external attack. In wrestling with the
tensions of social ideals and political realities, Hopkins had
a special gift that stood him well. Inevitably, he suffered
setbacks as legislation for his programs required compromise, as appropriations pared down budgetary requests, as
particular states or localities failed to observe to the letter
each step of relief policies. After each rebuff or defeat,
Hopkins was resilient; he would launch a fresh strategy or
try another tactic; but to an extraordinary degree he remained true to the core of his ideals and his designs.

Hopkins' impact on politics exceeded his marked success
in advancing specific programs. In the New Deal era and
beyond, he exerted a lasting influence upon political attitudes and thinking, upon the formulation and reformulation
of public values, upon governmental structures, and upon
bureaucratic processes in the social welfare field.

From the close of World War I to the New Deal there
was a long interval in which a strict construction of the
Constitution held sway. William Howard Taft's advocacy
of a literal reading of the document enjoyed its fullest
reign in that period and, so far as court holdings were concerned, literalism was not to terminate until well into
Roosevelt's Presidency, after the "Court-packing" crisis and

the creation of the "Roosevelt Court." The New Deal, of
course, required a liberal construction of the Constitution;
pioneering programs, such as Hopkins', stood among the
powerful engines that moved the country and ultimately
the Court away from traditional literalism. The Taftian
approach tended toward minimum domestic functions for
the national government, and a preference for state and
local action or, even more, for private initiative and enterprise. In his relief programs, Hopkins successfully com-
batted literal constitutionalism in dislodging the prepon-
derance of relief activity from its state, local, and private
moorings to fix it firmly upon a base of federal responsibility. His mammoth action programs were founded upon
premises of broad constitutional construction, contributing
a major force in the transformation of constitutional theory
during the New Deal era.

Hopkins was also a transformer of key ideas and attitudes of the political culture. He shifted public and official
thinking about social need—whether created by unemployment, illness, or other vicissitudes of life—from a stance of
ethical rigidity and stern judgment to a larger vision of
compassion and remedial action. To alter the political and
social culture, Hopkins had to combat religious and ethical
obstacles which had long and strong roots. The centuries-
old Protestant ethic, which enjoyed the widest currency in
American society, was a work ethic that attributed unemployment to the victim's inherent unworthiness; worst of
all, being unemployed was perceived as attributable to
indolence, and for those upon whom the tragedy fell it
was the badge of shame. Hopkins had to penetrate this wall
of cold repugnance and indifference. At least for the interval of the New Deal, he succeeded in implanting new
principles that embraced federal programs for the unemployed, a national social security program, and, above all,
the concept of society's responsibility for social disaster

and its victims—a concept most logically and fittingly expressed through federal public assistance programs. In effect, the punitive severities of the Protestant ethic began to be replaced by a sensitive Good Samaritan personified by national and, gradually, state and local governments.

Another element of the political culture with which Hopkins had to joust was the overwhelming ascendance in American society of the business community, to which politics was an adjunct. With utter accuracy and candor, Coolidge had said that "the business of America is business," and Hoover had expressed the same sentiment in slightly different phraseology. For those whom it could not or would not employ, business had almost indiscernible concern or conscience, and little more for the faithful employee who ultimately succumbed to age and pensionless retirement. Rugged individualism's sole concession to the victims of social Darwinism was private charity, a small-scale, spasmodic gesture toward human suffering, whose inadequacies were exposed quickly by the Depression. Traditional confidence in the businessman as the provider of prosperity was also shaken badly. The time was ripe to challenge allied beliefs. One of Hopkins' major contributions to the political philosophy of the New Deal inhered in his overriding the indifference of business to its own victims by establishing public programs, supported by newly formed, accepting attitudes at the various decision points of the American political structure.

Hopkins also had to face new trends in social and intellectual thought that were inhospitable to his relief program. Among the most powerful of these was the increasingly influential Freudian psychology, recently arrived from Europe and flourishing in its new environment from the 1920s onward. Its thrust was to concentrate on the individual and his inadequacies in seeking to understand the causes of his social and economic deprivations. Consequently, Freudian psychologists tended to overlook or minimize such environmental factors as economic forces or social conditions, which were the mainsprings of Hopkins' concepts and programs. Hopkins perceived that the dominant factors producing unemployment lay in the environment, and that therefore the direction of public programs must be toward an amelioration of these environmental factors. The individual was to be accepted as he was, and, so far as possible, work relief programs were to be aimed at giving expression to differences in individual talents and needs.

Finally, Hopkins and his programs contributed to alterations in the political system; to the differentiation between the governmental sector and the private sector of functions designed to alleviate social problems, vastly increasing the governmental role; and to functional distributions among the levels of government, with a vast net expansion of national activity. Hopkins was a major contributor to the enormous extension of the historic federal grant-in-aid device as a vehicle for social programs. Thereby, he largely structured the relief system on a foundation of broad political involvement and support, engaging the federal, state, and local governments in the enterprise of public assistance.

Hopkins, the New Dealer, made a lasting impact upon social and political history. His concept of relief was new and historic. According to Hopkins, relief, born of a social responsibility to meet a social problem, was most appropriately administered by a social agency rather than by a financial or other agency. This concept portended the social and humanitarian rather than financial connotation of relief.

Hopkins' approach provided the basis for a new flowering of the social work profession. Previously concentrated in

the local and private sectors and modest in scale, the profession—thanks chiefly to Hopkins and his programs—
became for the first time national in dimension. A kind of
social work explosion was necessary to provide the staff
for Hopkins' burgeoning programs. He was also largely
responsible for creating the first opportunity for the social
work profession to be represented regularly in Presidential
councils and, thereby, in the shaping of national social
policy.

Hopkins designed and effected the first massive public
works administration in American experience—a landmark
in public and social administration. The achievement
brought revolutionary proportions to social policy, ac-
knowledging a permanent responsibility of government for
the unemployed, and entrusting its fulfillment to professional hands—the social workers and administrators who
staffed his programs. Thus social work emerged from
minor circumscribed roles in public affairs to a status of
rapid ascendancy and dominion over central, large-scale
programs of the New Deal. This dominion has endured
and, indeed, has expanded as further social functions have
been undertaken by government.

The most enduring and consequential of Hopkins' contributions was his leadership in establishing the social
security system. He played the most active role in the
development of recommendations by a Presidential committee and, in fact, left an unfinished agenda for future
consideration: parts of his plan that were omitted in
Hopkins' day but were adopted later, and others that are
still being debated. It is not a rash contention that, ultimately, they will all be fulfilled.

By these contributions, Hopkins became a primary force
in the New Deal's development of a dual character. In its
initial stages, the New Deal was engrossed in economic recovery, in freeing the country from the pervasive hardships

of the Depression. Hopkins was guardian of the Depression's most suffering victims, the unprecedented masses of unemployed. The swift relief his programs brought them conveyed an understanding (in contrast to the Hoover era) that government cared for these victims and worked earnestly to relieve their plight. Hopkins' programs were not a mere exercise in symbolic politics, but brought concrete here-and-now benefits to the citizen. The success of Hopkins' and other programs enabled the New Deal to achieve the task of recovery and move into a second stage—reform. In essence, reform involved the adaptation of the inherited capitalistic system, with business dominance of government, to an affirmation that government and the political system were capable of independent decision and the acknowledgement that the federal government has a continuing responsibility for social welfare functions.

The Second, or Reform, New Deal had several major facets in whose development Hopkins shared. He was a principal counselor, insistent and persuasive, who induced an often-wavering Roosevelt to resort to deficit financing as a means of keeping the economy functioning at an acceptable tempo. In addition, Hopkins the reformer oriented federal programs toward the nation's growing urbanization by channeling relief aid from the federal government directly to the cities. Hopkins' other principal contributions to New Deal reform include: a comprehensive multipart plan for social security, the basis of the Social Security Act; the establishment of a national program of public works for relief of unemployment; and the implicit undertaking by the federal government of responsibility for coping with that eventuality.

For the rest, Hopkins made government attentive to forgotten people: to the Negro who historically had been invariably shortchanged by federal policy; to transients who were prey to the public attitude that they were the responsibility of no governmental jurisdiction; to the aged and the disabled. Most important of all, Hopkins moved mountains in bringing those millions who had been plunged suddenly into the despair of unemployment, innocent and unsuspecting of that oncoming danger, to a restoration or renewal of their faith in democracy and the political system.

If Hopkins were to reappear today, there is much in existing social policy that would trigger his blunt disapproval; and it would drive him to charge off into action. The prevailing approach to welfare programs, we can be sure, would horrify him: the denigrating public attitudes toward those who are unemployed or cannot work; the humiliating tests and procedures for determining eligibility; the punitive work requirements—"workfare" is a current word—with little, if any, attention to the quantity and quality of work and its specific suitability for the individual beneficiary; and the incredible philosophy of "benign neglect," articulated by Patrick Moynihan as adviser to President Nixon.

Since 1969, the Nixon administration, with fluctuating degrees of commitment, has been giving attention to "welfare reform." Yet after nearly five years of study and discussion, little discernible progress has been made. We have not had and are unlikely to have legislation for genuine welfare reform. There is confusion and disagreement over approaches and principles, and at the moment of this writing an utter impasse. It is not too much to suggest that present-day policy makers and planners would do well to consult the Hopkins role, philosophy, and accomplishments—doubtless the most rewarding interlude in American experience for the taxpaying public and the welfare recipient alike. From today's perspective, Hopkins' successes had a constructive spirit and accepting attitude, which did not look upon the welfare client as unworthy;

and it is safe to predict that until we develop a comparable
spirit of humanity, of restraint in allocating blame and in
withholding-penalties, little improvement in present-day
welfare problems will be made.

Hopkins' concept of work relief might also be helpful
today. To him, work was not a punitive device to redeem
oneself from Original Sin or indolence, as it is often still
considered today; rather, the art of relief administration is
the provision of work that is useful, that approximates the
talent of the unemployed, and that is rewarded with a cash
wage roughly comparable to that in private employment.
It is as easy now, perhaps easier, to see at every hand the
need for public works projects which, in the Nixon administration, have become only a minor weapon in the struggle
against unemployment. A walk in any city, in the rapidly
growing suburbs, or in the hidden areas of rural poverty
reveals a need for hundreds of Hopkins-like projects, administrators, and their legion of helpers. One's thoughts leap
at the vision of Hopkins today leading the unemployed in
public works efforts directed toward solving environmental
problems.

For us in the 70s, Hopkins remains the creator of an
unfinished agenda of social policy, including some items
that were germane to his own administration but have since
been diminished and debased. The school lunch program,
which he initiated, has been prey to pressure interests un-
friendly to its original premises. It needs review and restoration to the nutritional variety and instructional soundness
of Hopkins' day, and a return to an aspiration he had for
it—that it be "a device in social education." Most important
of all, the country still awaits and needs increasingly with
each passing year the kind of public insurance that Hopkins
considered the most valuable of all—national health insurance on a compulsory basis.

For the present-day administrator of social programs,

Hopkins remains an invaluable working model. He stands as a supreme achiever of results in complex political and bureaucratic milieus. He disdained that school of administrative practice which channels funds into overhead, offices, comfortable appointments for top leadership, allowances, and management studies. Hopkins took vows of administrative austerity; appropriations and benefits flowed to his clientele.

Today, Hopkins stands in contrast to the administrators of social programs in the Nixon era. These programs have been politicized, tied to strong White House control, with professional program administrators working within tightly circumscribed limits. A heavy imbalance favors political leadership at the expense of program leadership. Among the costs are grossly reduced innovation, abolition or sharp paring back of programs, and—thanks to the device of impoundment—enormous sums of Congressionally authorized but unspent funds which had been allocated by a sympathetic legislature. In contrast, Hopkins was the program professional who, with Presidential encouragement, developed political skill and power in his own right. Ultimately, he became a principal political protagonist of his flourishing programs in all political arenas.

Dr. Kurzman has provided us with the authoritative book on Hopkins' experience in and contribution to the New Deal. The author's net has been cast wide; he has utilized available manuscript collections, oral histories and interviews, Hopkins' own materials, and a vast body of secondary material.

For the student of social work and social history, this study presents a thorough view of a central figure of the American social work profession, at a point in time when both public attitudes toward social work (and social welfare) and the attitudes of the social work profession itself were being revolutionized. It is no exaggeration that the profession was being reborn or totally remade. Hopkins served as a principal agent and the New Deal as a principal arena for that transformation. In this book we witness a fundamental change in the social worker's self-image—of his function and place in the social and political systems.

For the social historian, the era of Hopkins and the New Deal is the interval of the most far-reaching innovations in social programs and policies that America has ever experienced. The concepts, the forces and obstacles, the nature of the achievements—all are explored in these pages.

The political scientist and political historian can witness here a social and political system, in the depths of national crisis, struggling to emerge by basic adaptations, wrought under overwhelming pressures and a cruelly short time limitation. Democracy was tested as never before by economic crisis; and this book provides an account and analysis of a major sector of successful effort to meet those tests.

Here students of public administration can observe how a program leader—Hopkins—struggled with a duality that has long intrigued scholars: politics and administration. Just before Hopkins' day in national affairs, public administration literature had dwelt upon the *separation* of these two areas. Hopkins' experience demonstrates how they are inextricably intertwined, and how a single administrator who combines singular skill in both arenas can attain masterly results. His New Deal career is virtually a case study of the ways an administrator, employing the resources and opportunities of both politics and administration, can maximize program impact and innovation. In addition, Hopkins' New Deal career coincides with a major transformation of public administration from a highly formalized study with fixed principles (detailed by Gulick and Urwick) to one of emphasis on organizational cooperation, soon to be articulated by Chester Barnard and a long procession of practitioners and scholars. Hopkins was truly a prototype of Barnard's public administrator.

For the student of political philosophy and process, Hopkins, in my judgment, represents the triumph of the *democratic* administrator. Despite the size and impersonality of bureaucracy and the complexities of politics, Hopkins' programs utilized to the fullest the structure of a democratic system, and the beneficiaries of those programs were dealt with in a democratic manner and spirit. These happy results occurred, most of all, because of the personal values of the program administrator—Harry Hopkins. Indeed my favorite observation by Hopkins, reported here by Dr. Kurzman, is that no recipient of social aid should be treated as an exile in his own country.

Louis W. Koenig
Professor of Government
New York University

Preface

THIS MODEST VOLUME makes no pretense at being the exhaustive work on Hopkins in the 1930s; that would be another task altogether. Rather, it represents an attempt to capture the spirit and achievements of the man: a social worker little remembered by his own profession, an able executive seldom studied in public administration, and a leader of a generation past, largely forgotten by the present generation. In an era where the Watergate scandal shadows the performance of an Administration, it may well be worthwhile to review the contributions of an innovator in government who resolutely set the highest standards of probity for himself and for all who worked with him.

In short, there is a need to reawaken social workers, public administrators, political and social scientists and historians, and concerned citizens generally to the unique political and social contributions of Harry Hopkins. Hopkins showed us that integrity and innovation can co-exist in government administration and that effective leadership can provide a basis for solving even the most vexing social problems. For the citizen whose tax money underwrites social welfare expenditures, the lesson may well be the same: that as a nation, we can profit from the insights, methods and achievements of a Harry Hopkins in the past, before charting new paths for public programs in the future.

It may surprise many readers that there is remarkably
little written by Hopkins, and very little more written by
others about him. Aside from Robert E. Sherwood's classic
study, *Roosevelt and Hopkins*, and Searle Charles' *Minister
of Relief*, there are only scattered articles in popular and
scholarly journals, and a few chapters referring to Hopkins
in books about the Depression. The Sherwood text is a
monumental effort, but it devotes only three of its thirty-
six chapters to Hopkins' years in relief administration; the
principal portion of the book is concerned with the relationship between Roosevelt and Hopkins during the
1940s after Hopkins had left social welfare service to par-
ticipate in the war effort. The Charles book is a fine historical summary of Hopkins' work during the 1930s, but
supplies relatively little insight into the nature of the contributions made by Hopkins in the sphere of social welfare
administration.

Harry Hopkins and the New Deal takes a different approach. It is concerned with the impact of the man upon
the social institutions of the 1930s, and with his influence
on the decision-making process of that decade in the very
highest echelons of government. In this respect, this is a
study by a professional public administrator and social
worker who is, as well, a student of government and political science.

Like most research, this study is not without biases
which inevitably affect its observations and conclusions.
First, as a professional social worker, the author's sym-
pathies are aligned with those who suffer and with those
men and women who spend the better part of their lives
in relieving distress. Hopkins was surely such a man. Second,
as a student of administration, the author is acutely aware
of the dilemmas of decision-making and the management
of public agencies in the context of a competitive political
system. Finally, Hopkins became inescapably almost an

extension of oneself—a part of the researcher's own life after "living" with him for so many months, night and day, weekdays and weekends. Ultimately, for this period the author spent as much time with this "stranger" as he had with his own friends and family. This fact cannot help engendering an element of identification. Given the conditions which Roosevelt and Hopkins faced in the 1930s, it was not hard for this identification to take place, and for a quality of empathy to enter into the research and evaluation process.

As C. Wright Mills once said, "I have tried to be objective. I do not claim to be detached." To contribute toward that objectivity, the author immersed himself in the published material on all sides of the contemporary issues: by those who favored Hopkins and those who did not; by historians who have condemned the New Deal, and those who have testified to its contributions; by the pro-Hoover, as well as the pro-Roosevelt; by the far-right as well as the far-left. In the end, one has to distinguish opinions from facts and weigh events in an objective framework. Every effort has been made to accomplish this, and complete citations to the many-sided documentation are offered.

Research involved an extensive review of both published material relevant to social welfare in the 1930s and original source material—much of the latter previously untapped. The books and articles used embrace a range of thought that runs from social work to economics, from public administration to sociology, from partisan politics to political science—to present a deliberately *interdisciplinary* approach to this inquiry. If this approach has been fruitful it is because the contributions and insights into the period are not the monopoly of any one profession or field of study—and certainly not that of the author.

Original source material has proved rich and rewarding. Documentary analysis involved four major collections:

the National Archives, the Library of Congress, the Oral
History Research Office at Columbia University, and the
Franklin D. Roosevelt Library at Hyde Park, N.Y.

The National Archives yielded a treasure of information,
demanding the patience to sift through seemingly endless
boxes of primary source material. Most useful for this study
were the correspondence files of the FERA, CWA, and
WPA organizations, which included the official correspondence of Hopkins and his principal deputies. This correspondence consists of internal letters and memoranda between staff and regional offices, as well as exchanges with
other agencies of government, the White House, Congress,
and social welfare agencies in the private sector. In addition,
the Archives made available a complete set of the monthly
reports of those agencies, their chronological summaries,
and well over half of Hopkins' unpublished speeches delivered during his tenure as administrator of relief.

The Library of Congress Manuscript Division holds the
collections of two of the most influential social welfare
leaders of the period, John A. Kingsbury and Sophonisba
P. Breckinridge. Because of the former's particularly close
personal and professional relationship with Hopkins, his
papers were extraordinarily helpful in separating wheat
from chaff regarding the rumors and allegations that per-
tained to Hopkins' work during the 1930s. Miss Breckinridge's papers were useful in tracing Hopkins' relationship
to the social work profession and social work education,
since she enjoyed immense prestige in both areas. The
important reciprocal influence of Hopkins on social work
has been documented here largely through her papers, together with the other source documents which those papers,
in turn, suggested. In addition, the manuscripts of the President's Research Committee on Social Trends were consulted to document some of the developing social welfare
policies in the latter part of the decade.

The Oral History Research Office at Columbia University is a goldmine of information unduplicated by other sources. The collection is comprised of carefully structured, tape-recorded interviews, conducted by experienced historians with selected public leaders. Transcribed and edited, these interviews are made available in loose-leaf albums. Extensive use was made of the volumes relating to the special Social Security Project, including interviews with Eveline Burns, Jane Hoey, and Frank Bane. The author was especially fortunate to have been among the first researchers to have access to these papers, since the collection had not been open to public inspection until the spring of 1970. In addition, several other collections, not part of the Social Security Project, were found to be equally helpful: the taped interviews with Arthur Krock, Rexford Tugwell, and Paul Appleby. Unfortunately, the interviews with Henry Wallace and Frances Perkins will remain closed until 1975; they should prove a valuable source of study for future scholars of this period.

The Franklin D. Roosevelt Library at Hyde Park was a principal source of documents, including the well-organized collection of the original manuscripts of both Roosevelt and Hopkins. The entire Hopkins collection was reviewed: his official public papers for 1933-1938; his personal, private papers (on microfilm) for 1931-1940; and the eighteen bound volumes of news clippings for 1933-1938, which contain approximately 3,600 pages of articles from all parts of the nation on Hopkins and on the work of the relief administrations.

Research at Hyde Park also included the collection of Roosevelt's Papers as Governor (1928-1932), which revealed valuable source material on Hopkins' early relationship with Roosevelt and the operations of New York State's Temporary Emergency Relief Administration (TERA). In addition, portions of Roosevelt's Papers as President,

Official file, and the President's Secretary's File, were examined, particularly for the years 1933-1938. Also useful were the smaller collections of the papers of Aubrey Williams, Hopkins' principal deputy in the WPA, and of Rexford Tugwell, whose insights as a Brains Trust member were clearly influential on both Roosevelt and Hopkins.

At the Roosevelt Library, the author also consulted the papers of Paul Appleby, whose influence on administration went far beyond his formal post as Executive Assistant to the Secretary of Agriculture. The Frances Perkins papers, although limited in number, include a valuable collection of drafts of articles and position papers on plans for social security, which have handwritten marginal notations that are as useful as the formal materials themselves.

In May 1973, the Roosevelt Library opened many additional papers in the Harry Hopkins Collection, revealing new material which has been incorporated in this study. An excellent new card index to the three principal Presidential Collections (Official, Personal, and Secretary's Files), identifying a wealth of Hopkins material, was utilized.

In addition to analysis of these documents, the author conducted a limited number of personal interviews with leading figures of the 1930s who knew Hopkins. They included Luther Gulick, Raymond Moley, Frank Bane, Louis Koenig, and the late Samuel I. Rosenman. Correspondence with Elizabeth Wisner, Rexford Tugwell, Robert K. Straus, and others, as well as with the archivists at the New York State Library's Manuscript and History Collection, and at the Library of Grinnell College, Hopkins' *Alma Mater,* produced much helpful material. Some of the "interviews by correspondence" involved an exchange of cassette tapes, embodying special questions for each interview and, in return, his or her responses. This system proved quite productive;

interviewees seemed much more receptive to answering at length by tape rather than by lengthy, typewritten letters.

Several of the more important annual publications of the period were consulted, including the *Proceedings* of the National Conference of Social Work (1929-1938), *Municipal Yearbooks* (1937-1939), *Social Work Year Books* (1933, 1935, 1937, 1939), and *Annals* of the American Academy of Political and Social Science for the 1930s (selectively, by index). Testimony in the *Congressional Record* on unemployment and relief (73d-75th sessions of Congress), the monthly reports of the FERA and WPA, and relevant *Reports* and *Hearings* of Committees of Congress studying proposed legislation and appropriations also yielded important information.

Pertinent articles and editorials of the *New York Times* were reviewed extensively—a task made manageable by that newspaper's excellent index. The leading periodicals of the era, such as *Time, Newsweek, Literary Digest, Collier's, Harper's, Today, Survey, New Republic, American Magazine, Social Service Review, Nation* and *Fortune* were consulted selectively.

Virtually every article that Hopkins himself ever wrote, and most of those written about him during his tenure as administrator of relief (1933-1938), found largely in the bound volumes of newspaper clippings in the Hyde Park collection, supplied a vast amount of firsthand information and contemporary assessments of Hopkins. This source was supplemented by extensive research to unearth articles, often unindexed, in professional journals and regional publications.

The several individuals who assisted immeasurably in the research process or in the totality of this study will be found in the *Acknowledgements*. All of them concurred with the author's conviction that Hopkins' many contributions to American life should be recorded permanently

for the appreciation and profit of present and future generations.

                                        Paul A. Kurzman

School of Social Work
Columbia University
New York, N. Y.
January 1974

Acknowledgements

MANY PERSONS demonstrated their eagerness to assist in the research for this study of Harry Hopkins. First, a word of appreciation is due to the staffs of the many library and document collections which were consulted—in particular, to the remarkably resourceful archivists of the Franklin D. Roosevelt Library at Hyde Park, N.Y. Second, a great debt of gratitude is acknowledged to those men and women who knew Hopkins in the 1930s, and were willing to take time out from their busy schedules to grant interviews and conduct correspondence.

This study has gained greatly from the wise counsel of three thoughtful readers, Dr. Charlton Chute, Dr. Helen Hilling and Dr. Eveline M. Burns.

Dr. Chute gave generously of his time for guidance toward the most fruitful and productive avenues of research, patiently sharing his wealth of experience with governmental programs—federal, state and local.

Dr. Hilling, a mentor throughout the course of the inquiry, provided an invaluable perspective on developments in social welfare, based upon her many years of experience as a social work administrator and theoretician. Her advice assisted greatly in integrating social welfare with public administration.

Dr. Burns' perceptive comments and review of this

manuscript in early 1973 served to strengthen the text and suggested important new references for research.

Gratitude should also be extended to the anonymous faculty committee at New York University which saw fit to confer upon the original manuscript the annual Martin E. Dworkis Memorial Award for distinguished scholarship in the field of public administration.

The initial research was conducted under a fellowship (CH 35-436) from the Research and Development Branch of the National Center for Health Services, U.S. Public Health Service, Washington, D.C. This support made it possible to conduct research on a full-time basis during portions of two years.

Finally, I acknowledge especially the quiet contribution of my wife, Margaret, and daughter, Katherine. My wife's understanding of my wish to undertake this research made it possible for me to work with equanimity throughout. She has been a patient and supportive partner in this venture, and has lent her artistic creativity in designing the dust jacket for this book. As for my daughter, Katherine, and my son, David—their mere presence in this world fills every day of my life with inspiration, warmth and joy.

Without the help of all these persons—unnamed or named—this book might not have been written; but, for good or ill, I alone must be held accountable for the final product.

P.A.K.

Introduction

A sound leader's aim
Is to open people's hearts,
Fill their stomachs,
Calm their wills,
Brace their bones,
And so to clarify their thoughts and
*   cleanse their needs*
That no cunning meddler could
*   touch them:*
Without being forced, without strain
*   or constraint,*
Good government comes of itself.

Lao Tzu
6th Century B.C.

HARRY HOPKINS IS AN ENIGMA. One would expect
to find much written about him, if only because he
personally spent more public money in the 1930s than had
any other man before him in American history. Yet too
little is written and too little is known. Ironically, when
Hopkins is remembered—if he is remembered at all—it is
for his contributions as presidential advisor during World
War II. Perhaps this should not surprise us, for his war role

was much more glamorous, involving face-to-face negotia-
tions with such world leaders as Churchill and Stalin. It
was less controversial, as well, for here Hopkins was in a
staff role, relieved from the responsibilities of line administration involving daily decision-making and the spending
of taxpayers' money.

For a man who is said to have been one of the most
powerful administrators in recent history, little scholarly
research and publication are available. Lesser known
figures—in government and the professions—have proved
far more popular subjects for study. There are several
practical explanations. First, Hopkins himself wrote so
little, and much of what bears his name appears to have
been ghostwritten, including the major portion of his book,
Spending to Save. [1]   Even taking the book at face value
tells us little about Hopkins, the man, or Hopkins, the
administrator. A disproportionate amount of the book is
devoted to the inadequate efforts of the Hoover administration, and only about eighty to ninety pages to the
operation of the FERA, CWA and WPA. Published in mid-
October of 1936, it must be regarded, in part, as a partisan
political document in criticism of Hoover and in defense
of the policies of the Roosevelt administration. It is hardly,
as the subtitle states, "The Complete Story of Relief." [2]

Second, Hopkins did not keep an extensive diary as did
Ickes and Morgenthau. Such diaries always invite biographers, for they inevitably are rich in detailed recollections
and factual notation. Perhaps Hopkins was too busy to
keep a diary; or, aware of his poor writing skills, he may
have resisted doing so. He spoke forcefully and well, but
his writing was heavy and labored. "When he talked, his
language was extraordinarily vivid and original and to the
point," notes Robert Sherwood. "When he wrote for publication, he was apt to become self-conscious, sententious
and awkward." [3]

Third, Hopkins' wartime service as head of Lend Lease and resident White House adviser was more glamorous, less controversial—and, in many ways, eclipsed his relief work of the 1930s. No one has seriously disputed his devoted service to Roosevelt during the early 1940s and most historians, in fact, have found that Hopkins was a sort of "folk hero" during those difficult days of wartime negotiation.

Fourth, historians and biographers traditionally have been attracted toward study of the presidency, and particularly to the administration of Franklin D. Roosevelt. Inevitably, those studies lead to an analysis of the role of Hopkins as an adviser to Roosevelt, and thus many articles (and chapters of several books) are devoted to Harry Hopkins, man in the White House.

Finally, Hopkins died young—at the age of 55—which precluded his having time to write his memoirs, as publishers surely would have convinced him to do. Nor was he available for researchers to interview, or for a role as elder statesman of the famous Roosevelt administration. He left the public scene as quietly and inconspicuously as he had entered, and few scholars have taken the time to discern the importance of his numerous contributions in the crucial years of the Depression.

The goal of this book is to begin to fathom these waters; to study the man and his lasting imprint on social policy and social welfare administration. In this regard, it will map his contributions to the formation of public welfare policy during the 1930s. This is not a study per se of WPA, or of any of the other alphabet agencies which Hopkins administered. Nor is this a biography of Hopkins' life. Rather, it is an analysis of the role which Hopkins played in the arena from 1931 to 1938, and its enduring impact on the American people and their social and political institutions.

It is recognized that a dramatic change took place in social welfare policy and administration during the 1930s— a movement that one might term "from poor law to public welfare." It is the hypothesis of this study that Harry Hopkins played a principal role in effecting this change, both as a *formulator* of the new policy and as an *executor* of policy to which official sanction had been given. Thus, it views Hopkins both as architect and builder, and as designer and engineer. In assuming these roles Hopkins may have been one of the major (and largely unrecognized) figures in shaping the modern public social policy that emerged from the Depression.

If this hypothesis is valid, Hopkins should take his place among the ranks of great leaders in social history. Patrick Anderson has noted, however, that this is not the case today. He suggests that many members of the current generation, "asked to identify Harry Hopkins, would venture a guess that he once played shortstop for the Cardinals." [4] If true, it is a tragic commentary on the nature of our scholarly investigation. For if Harry Hopkins were one of the most influential social welfare administrators of this century, then this should be documented and made known so that he can take his rightful place in American history.

NOTES

1. Confirmation of the fact that most of Hopkins' published writings were ghostwritten is available from his manuscripts in the Roosevelt Library Collection. In a transcribed telephone conversation between Hopkins and his assistant, Corrington Gill, for example, Gill replies to Hopkins: "I don't feel I ought to pass on my views to you of the manuscript of your book because it's so obviously not *yours*. . . . none of the chapters sound like you." (September 15, 1936, Hopkins Personal Papers, Roosevelt Library Collection.) Furthermore,

' Paul Appleby confirms that Hopkins' article for *The American Magazine,* like many others, was actually ghostwritten. (Oral History Research Office, Columbia University, Appleby MSS, p. 155.) Among those who drafted articles and speeches for Hopkins were Arthur E. Burns, an economist for WPA, and Cabell Phillips, an information officer for the WPA, 1935-1938.

2. For a thoughtful, critical review of Hopkins' book see Edith Abbott, "Book Reviews," *Social Service Review*, X (December, 1936), pp. 684-88.

3. Robert E. Sherwood, *Roosevelt and Hopkins: An Intimate History* (rev. ed., New York: Harper and Bros., 1950), pp. 18-19.

4. Patrick Anderson, *The Presidents' Men* (Garden City, N.Y.: Doubleday and Co., 1968), p. 6.

Part I

THE SETTING FOR REFORM

The basis of successful relief in national distress is to mobilize and organize the infinite number of agencies of self-help in the community. That has been the American way of relieving distress among our own people and the country is successfully meeting its problem in the American way today.

Herbert Hoover

And it ought to be remembered that there is nothing more difficult to take in hand, more perilous to conduct, or more uncertain in its success, than to take the lead in the introduction of a new order of things.

Niccolo Machiavelli

I. The Philosophy of Relief Administration

American Poor Law

FROM THE 18th century through 1929 there were few major changes in public relief methods in the United States. Basic relief was provided under state "poor laws" which charged localities with primary responsibility for care of their destitute and needy. During the early years of the 20th century, in several states growing dissatisfaction with conditions prevailing under poor laws had resulted in passage of supplementary relief legislation provided categorical relief to such "worthy" poor as the aged, disabled, blind, and young mothers with dependent children. Assistance to the blind had been enacted in twenty-two states, but aid to the aged in only ten. In contrast, veterans' relief legislation had been enacted in forty-four states, for there was a feeling that they had made a special sacrifice for the country and, therefore, were more "worthy" poor. All but five states had some provisions for aid to dependent children in their own homes and all but three had statutes concerning the care of dependent children in foster homes and institutions. [1]

The situation was even more desolate than statistics alone might portray. As late as 1929, the almshouse was still the chief means of caring for the poor. In some states care of the poor was let out to the lowest bidder; destitute children were indentured or apprenticed to those who could support them; applicants for relief were required to take the degrading "pauper's oath" by which they swore to their condition of absolute destitution; relatives who had "sufficient ability" could be called upon to support their poor and, if they refused, could be prosecuted and fined or placed in prison; and, as late as 1934, the constitutions of fourteen states deprived relief recipients of the right to vote and to hold office. [2]

This local system of public relief was supplemented by the philanthropic activities of various private charities, the churches, sectarian provisions, and certain wealthy individuals. While private (voluntary) social agencies were to be found throughout the United States, they were concentrated in the large cities and the industrialized states. Private charity, therefore, was not a potent factor in the rural states, especially those of the South and Southwest. Private charitable agencies often were affiliated financially through Community Chest organizations or Health and Welfare Councils, and a modicum of coordination was achieved through various councils of social agencies.

Experience in England

The United States came into the Depression with a public assistance program still grounded in the law and social philosophy of the Elizabethan Poor Law of 1601. In this respect, America was several generations behind the countries of western Europe, including England itself. As Grace Abbott notes,

> What is surprising is that...the policies of the Elizabethan poor law have been modified so little, or in many places not at all, and that we should have

continued to cherish old policies after the English themselves had altered or discarded them. [3] During the late 19th and early 20th centuries, marked modifications had taken place in England to bring the Poor Law of 1601 up to date. Cash had been substituted for much of the earlier relief "in kind," and much of the emphasis on making relief unacceptable by surrounding it with hardships and humiliations had been swept aside. But our public welfare laws remained, Joanna Colcord observes, "like flies embalmed in amber, a memorial to a vanished social-economic pattern." [4]

Public and Private Involvement

While public relief remained a town and village responsibility throughout most of the country, it generally was under the supervision of untrained "overseers of the poor" who were best known for their political credentials. Since local governments had to administer and finance their own poor relief, the allocations were niggardly, both for staff and recipients. In no sense could the public sector claim to have a public welfare *program*. There was simply an attempt to sustain the "worthy" poor as cheaply and with as little administrative overhead and corruption as possible.

The belief in the superiority of private over public relief was strongly felt and clearly voiced by the social work profession. This widespread conviction was held by the early private charity organization societies founded in this country after the Depression of 1873, and was probably in large measure an understandable reaction to the spread of abuse and corruption in public relief during this period. With this historical evidence, the private charity organizations were able to make a convincing argument that it

was useless to try to reform public administration and
that, therefore, "outdoor relief" (relief outside the almshouse) should be abandoned. [5]   It *was* abolished during
the last quarter of the 19th century in eight of the largest
cities in the country, not to be restored again in most of
them until the beginning of the Depression of 1929. [6]

It is not surprising to find that social welfare agencies
generally were openly in favor of the conservative approach
of providing aid to the unemployed and needy through the
private sector. Moreover, wide dissemination of arguments
in favor of private charity and against public relief—expressed by such leaders as Mary Richmond, Francis McLean,
Josephine Lowell and Seth Low—had conditioned public
opinion to continue to rely on the voluntary sector for the
provision of relief. [7]

Factors Influencing Rejection of Public Relief

The rejection of a full-scale program of public relief at the
beginning of the Depression was no accident. The causes
can be traced through the development of thought and
ideology in the nation. Briefly, one can perceive these in-
fluences in at least five ways: political, religious, social,
economic and psychological.

The political preference for reliance on the private sector
is as old as the Founding Fathers and as recent as the 1955
report of the Kestnbaum Commission. [8]   Confidence in
the private sector is "the American way," and is not just a
20th century phenomenon. With this political philosophy
has gone a strong preference for localism, and a fear, if not
distaste, for federal intervention. Americans, therefore, had
steadfastly chosen localism in the administration and finance of relief; their preference here was entirely consistent
with their philosophy of government in other matters.

This political posture went hand-in-hand with a strict construction of the Constitution. For example, in the 1850s Dorothea Dix made a reasoned appeal for a grant of land to support the indigent insane. Her appeal was couched in persuasive terms. Congress passed the bill but President Pierce vetoed it on constitutional grounds. "The question presented," he wrote, "...is upon the constitutionality and propriety of the Federal Government assuming to enter into a novel and vast field of legislation, namely, that of providing for the care and support of all those among the people of the United States, who by any form of calamity, become fit objects of public philanthropy." [9]   As Sophonisba Breckinridge noted, this tone and message guided the political tenor of federal relief policy for more than three-quarters of a century, and was not reversed until the Federal Emergency Relief Act legislation was signed in 1933, and a new political stance toward federal involvement became effective. [10]

Our religious heritage was a second factor closely related to the above. Strongly influenced by our Puritan forefathers, President Hoover was comfortable in using his 1931 Lincoln's Day Address to say that he would reject pleas for national assistance in order "to avoid the opiates of government charity and the stifling of our national spirit of mutual self-help." Perhaps even more deeply imbedded in our beliefs was the Protestant ethic and the spirit of Calvinism. While the Protestant ethic would enable one to attribute poverty to indolence and lack of thrift, Calvinism provided the doctrines of total depravity, limited atonement and predestination. Dependency commonly was seen, therefore, as resulting solely from the fault of the dependent. "For as economic prosperity became the mark of the Lord's approval and poverty a sign that the victim has incurred His anger, it followed that those too poor to live without alms must be sinners in need of punishment. This

view of dependency was secularized and persisted long after
its underlying religious sanctions had lost their validity."
[11]

As religion provided a yardstick to measure the degree of
moral strength of the people, in turn, the social philosophy
of rugged individualism put a premium on "going it alone".
America had been a pioneer country, and the belief in
individualism was deeply rooted in the minds of men.
Little attention was paid to the social realities which the
individual had to face in a highly industrialized and fiercely
competitive society.

When the situation became urgent, this American philosophy therefore supported voluntarism over public charity.
Unlike public charity, personal and voluntary provision was
a favor and not a legal obligation, which therefore could be
suspended when it was deemed right and proper. In addition, the very notion of voluntarism, as de Tocqueville
observes perceptively, always has been a particularly American predilection and, hence, was the naturally preferred
response for the majority of the American people.

Psychological arguments also were prevalent. The 1920s
marked the arrival of Freudian psychology to the helping
professions and to cocktail party conversation. As the turn-
of-the-century reformers had emphasized the effects of an
adverse environment upon the individual, now the emphasis turned again to the inadequacies of the individual.
Where poor housing or discrimination had been blamed
a generation earlier, now defects in psycho-sexual development and the superego were held increasingly to blame.
The emphasis upon the individual and the consequent refusal to face harsh social and economic facts were, however, not the exclusive province of social workers; it was
the vogue that was reflected in the popular literature and
social conversation. Perhaps Freudianism should not have
been so influential a factor—especially in the decision-

making capitals of the Northeast—but the feeling among many was that the answer to joblessness and destitution lay not so much in a new political and social philosophy as it did in a few good years of analysis, not available of course to the poor.

A final factor influencing the rejection of public relief was the economic philosophy of the era. A premium was placed upon noninterference, not only by the physiocrats of an earlier age, but by the current leaders of industry who held power over the wealth of the country. The natural order of events should prevail, they argued, and therefore the government should take a laissez-faire position with regard to economic and social issues.

The views of the early 19th century political economist Thomas Malthus fitted well into the prevailing pattern and spoke directly to the issue of social welfare. Malthus argued that the population multiplied faster than the means of subsistence, and that unless the population were checked by a Darwinian "natural selection," poverty was inevitable. Hence, efforts by the government to sustain those who were not fit enough to provide for themselves only contributed to the population problem and increased the number of dependents who ought, instead, to be "selected" out. Therefore, Malthus urged the abandonment of public relief. The destitute man, he argued, ought to be left to the "uncertain support of private charity." The poor were responsible for their own misery and destitution, and had absolutely no right of claim on society. There was, in effect, no public responsibility. Whatever charity might be offered would be voluntary, out of pity, and even this, in fact, should be modest, temporary and restrained. [12]

The condition of relief policy in 1929 therefore does not lend itself to a simple explanation. Many factors, contemporary and historical, were at work in framing the policies that existed. Behind these policies was a world

view of that era that can be understood in terms of its
political, religious, social, psychological and economic
aspects. [13]

Thus it is not too surprising that the principles embodied
in the English Poor Law of 1601 and the interpretation
President Pierce had given to the "welfare clause" of the
Constitution in 1854 were still in effect in 1929. These
principles of Social Darwinism were inherited by Herbert
Hoover. Since they shaped much of his political philosophy,
they, in turn, were mirrored in many of his social programs.
Poor relief, he held, should be local, private, minimal and
deterrent.

NOTES

1. See Edward A. Williams, *Federal Aid for Relief* (New York:
Columbia University Press, 1939), p. 12, Arthur E. Burns and
Edward A. Williams, *Federal Work, Security and Relief Programs*
(Washington: U.S. Government Printing Office, 1941), p. 14.

2. Kathleen Woodroofe, *From Charity to Social Welfare* (Toronto: University of Toronto Press, 1966), p. 154.

3. Grace Abbott, *From Relief to Social Security: The Development of the New Public Welfare Services and Their Administration*
(Chicago: University of Chicago Press, 1941), p. 6.

4. Joanna C. Colcord, *Cash Relief* (New York: Russell Sage
Foundation, 1936), p. 11.

5. Josephine C. Brown, *Public Relief, 1929-1939* (New York:
Henry Holt and Co., 1940), p. 40. One of the reasons for establishing the New York Bureau of Municipal Research in 1906 was to make
government more efficient so it could begin to undertake modern
public programs without waste or corruption. See Jane S. Dahlberg,
The New York Bureau of Municipal Research: Pioneer in Government Administration (New York: New York University Press, 1966).

6. The cities were New York, Brooklyn, Baltimore, St. Louis,
Philadelphia, Washington, San Francisco and Kansas City. See Fred
R. Johnson, "Public Agencies for Needy Families," *Social Work Year
Book: 1929* (New York: American Association of Social Workers,
1929).

7. See Brown, *Public Relief.*

8. The Kestnbaum Report, in part, concludes that one should "leave to private initiative all the functions that citizens can perform privately" and "use the level of government closest to the community for all public functions it can handle." See *Final Report of the Commission on Intergovernmental Relations* (Washington: U.S. Government Printing Office, 1955), p. 6.

9. *Congressional Globe,* 33d Cong., 1st Sess., May 3, 1854, pp. 1061-63.

10. Sophonisba P. Breckinridge, *Public Welfare Administration in the United States* (Chicago: University of Chicago Press, 1938), pp. 222-24.

11. Helen Wright, "Dependency," in *Encyclopedia of the Social Sciences.* ed., Edwin Seligman (New York: Macmillan, 1931), V, pp. 93-95.

12. See Thomas R. Malthus, *An Essay on the Principle of Population* (Homewood, Ill.: R. D. Irwin, 1963).

13. It should be understood that religion was the basis of social and political philosophy and of political programs. As such, religion provided the unifying theme to the social, psychological and economic thought that comprised the *weltanschauung* of the era.

2. The Hoover Period: "Prosperity is just around the corner"

The Crisis

IN OCTOBER 1929, the stock market collapsed, and the consequences were felt throughout the nation. The boom of the 1920s had come to an abrupt halt at the very end of the decade. It was not long before the economic and social indicators made clear to all who were willing to listen that something very serious was happening throughout the land, not only to industry, but to the people. By the end of November—just one month after the market had fallen—nearly 3,000,000 people found themselves unemployed. [1]

President Hoover met with the leaders of business and industry. Through the U.S. Chamber of Commerce, he called on all industrial leaders to stimulate repairs and replacements, place advance orders through their retail and wholesale trade associations, promote prudent construction and set up information centers to offset the unfounded rumors about the business situation. Meanwhile, government officials and the captains of industry attempted to reassure a bewildered people. "Prosperity," they said, "is just around the corner."

During 1930, the problem grew increasingly worse. In spite of the facts—statistical and human—Hoover felt that the economy was essentially sound. In his message to Congress on December 2, 1930, the President underlined that the "fundamental strength of the Nation's economic life is unimpaired," and attributed the depression to speculative activity within our borders and to worldwide overproduction of basic commodities. [2] He urged employers not to cut payrolls or discharge workers, but this request was equivalent to asking the entire corporate structure to become a philanthropic machine.

By the early months of 1931, the United States Senate was attempting to create a system of direct federal relief. It had witnessed more than a year of growing unemployment and human suffering, and felt that the country had to respond. President Hoover was startled by the possibility of such legislation, and on February 3, 1931, he made a clear statement of his policies to an attentive press:

> This is not an issue as to whether people shall go hungry or cold in the United States. It is solely a question of the best method by which hunger and cold shall be prevented. It is a question as to whether the American people on the one hand will maintain the spirit of charity and mutual self-help through voluntary giving and the responsibility of local government as distinguished; on the other hand, from appropriating out of the Federal Treasury for such purposes. My own conviction is strongly that if we break down this sense of responsibility of individual generosity to individual and mutual self-help in the country in times of national difficulty and if we start appropriations of this character we have not only impaired something infinitely valuable in the life of the American people but have struck at the root of self-government. [3]

Reflecting on the President's statement, Silas Strong, president of the U.S. Chamber of Commerce added, "It would be deplorable if this country ever voted a dole. When we do that, we've hit the toboggan as a nation." [4]   Under these pressures, the proposed Senate legislation died as quietly as it was born.

Establishing Committees

In lieu of appropriations, Hoover decided to establish a committee. With unemployment having climbed to 5,500,000 by the end of 1930, the President appointed Colonel Arthur Woods of New York "to deal with the unemployment situation" through a "President's Emergency Committee for Employment." [5]   It decided to organize a nationwide regional organization to put two and one-half million people back to work for the winter of 1930-31. The Woods Committee was not successful mainly because it was not organized to render financial aid to the states and localities; instead, it merely furnished each state with the benefit of the experience of other states in coping with the unemployment problem. [6]   It was like the blind leading the blind.

After less than a year of operation, the Woods Committee was superceded by a new organization appointed by President Hoover, called the President's Organization on Unemployment Relief. Popularly known as the Gifford Committee (after its chairman, A.T.&T. President Walter S. Gifford), this successor organization had goals which were much the same as the Woods Committee but a significantly different name—no longer "Employment," but "Relief"—the ugly word. It was charged with mobilizing and coordinating voluntary fund-raising efforts in local communities throughout the nation. Despite its name, the organization made no effort to deal with the economic problem of unemployment and almost none to extend relief to the jobless. [7]

Despite the significant change in the names of the Committees (i.e., from "Employment" to "Relief"), in effect there was little difference between the Woods and Gifford Committees with respect to the basic issue of the proper role to be played by the federal government in alleviating unemployment and distress. Both were predicated on the assumption that the states and localities were responsible for unemployment relief and that direct federal financial aid was un-American and unwise. In spite of growing unemployment of crisis proportions, as late as December 1931, Gifford continued to place a strong emphasis on local financing and administration of all relief measures. Advancing "up the governmental ladder" to the county, he asserted, was unwise; bringing the state into the relief picture was even worse, and federal aid was virtually unthinkable. [8]

Gifford's approach finally brought the President's Organization on Unemployment Relief to the point of undisguised public embarrassment. Senators Costigan and LaFollette, long skeptical of Hoover's policies toward unemployment relief, brought Gifford before their Senate Subcommittee in January 1932. Senator Costigan lead the discussion with Gifford—presumably the nation's best-informed authority on relief—which went, in part, as follows:

> Senator Costigan: Do you know or does anyone else whom you can turn to know what the relief needs are in the smaller cities of the country which have no Community Chest organization?

Mr. Gifford:	No, I do not know.
Senator C.:	Do you know what the relief needs are in the rural districts of the United States?
Mr. G.:	No.
Senator C.:	Your Committee has not assembled information of this sort?
Mr. G.:	That is correct.
Senator C.:	Did you turn to the Red Cross for information?
Mr. G.:	Yes, we have some reports from the Red Cross.
Senator C.:	Did they supply you with any definite information as to the needs of the country as a whole?
Mr. G.:	No.
Senator C.:	Did you, from any other source, acquire information which would enable you specifically to advise us how many people in the United States at this hour are on the verge of starvation?

Mr. G.:   I have no such information.
                                 [9]

The President's Committee did not receive any further
Congressional appropriations; soon it, too, quietly died.

From Bad to Worse

Like all problems that are left largely unattended, the unemployment situation became worse with the passage of
time. By March 1932, at least 10,000,000 American workers
were idle, nearly double the figure of 5,500,000 that faced
Hoover only eighteen months before. By now the funds
raised through the voluntary sector—the Red Cross and
Community Chest campaigns—were all but exhausted.
Given the magnitude of the problem, the voluntary institutions were no longer practical instruments for relief even
in the communities that were less severely affected. Moreover, the reliance on local initiative meant that the overwhelming portion of the monies for relief came not from
voluntary contributions, but from the public funds of the
local communities themselves. Since these monies are
raised principally through real estate and property taxes,
continued local taxation drained the last pennies from
those who were already under an unreasonable financial
burden. Meanwhile, the large corporations were being
spared the effects of increased corporate taxation that had
the potential not only for greater equity but for tapping a
larger pool of available monies. Local relief meant making
the small homeowner pay. This policy was part of a pattern
of shielding concentrated wealth—a policy which many felt
helped to bring on the Depression in the first place. As one
small homeowner said, "I don't mind helping, but this just
doesn't seem fair."

The Government Reluctantly Intervenes

After vetoing earlier federal relief legislation, President
Hoover finally realized that the pressures for some form of
national assistance were too strong to be resisted any
longer. It was 1932; 10,000,000 workers were unemployed
and it was an election year for Hoover, who was running
for a second term. Many of those 10,000,000 Americans
would be going to the ballot box in November.

On July 21, 1932 the President signed into law the
Emergency Relief and Construction Act as a first step along
the road to federal involvement in unemployment relief.
[10]   The act contained three major titles but only the
first dealt directly with relief. [11]   It made available
$300,000,000 which the Reconstruction Finance Corpo-
ration (RFC) would advance to the states or their political
subdivisions at three percent annual interest for direct relief
or work relief for destitute persons. No outright federal
grants to the states would be made—only loans for self-
liquidating projects. If the states did not pay back the loans
on time, with interest, the unpaid monies would be deducted from their federal highway construction funds in
the years to follow. Even with these stringent provisions,
Hoover made it publicly clear that he was signing the legislation with great reluctance and only because it had been
"forced upon the government by the Democratic congressional leaders." [12]

The "loan" provision was, in effect, little more than a
face-saver, for he knew politically that, once the twenty-
fifth state (that is, then making a majority) took out a loan
the funds never would be repaid and that the federal government never would be able to deduct the money from state
highway funds. [13]   The act remained as the only federal
relief measure passed during the Hoover administration, and
it enabled Republican opponents of federal relief grants to

claim proudly that, because of the self-liquidating principle involved in the loan provision, the Act did not embody the concept of federal responsibility. They stressed that the legislation did not overthrow but, rather, facilitated the American system of local responsibility, and that the localities thereby were assisted in discharging their traditional relief function. [14]

A Billion Dollar Misunderstanding

In the agony that took place in these early years of the Depression, President Hoover showed that he misunderstood two of the most fundamental tenets of the American system. First, he failed to understand federalism and the Constitution; and second, he did not comprehend the will of the common man who ultimately governs in a democracy.

Hoover had said that the "inchoate new deal" propounded by Roosevelt would "undermine and destroy the American system" and "crack the timbers of the Constitution." He took a rigid, Newtonian approach toward the art of government and the process of social change. In this sense, perhaps it is true that he was a 19th century man. What Hoover failed to realize is that as society evolves, so must its means of governing; indeed, even its Constitution must be reinterpreted in the light of changing conditions. In fact, the timbers of the Constitution are more likely to break if they stay rigid than if they bend with the changing winds. What had to be done—which Hoover simply could not convince himself to do—was to permit the branches of the tree to bend, flexibly, while the tree itself remained deeply rooted.

Hoover resisted. "Change in the Constitution can and must be brought about only by the straightforward methods provided in the Constitution itself," said Hoover; "...the

Republican party denies the right of anyone to seek to
destroy the purposes of the Constitution by indirection."
[15]

In addition to viewing federal action for relief as contrary to the dictates of the Constitution, Hoover felt that
federal aid was inconsistent with the proper role of the
national government in a federal system. In his annual
Lincoln's Day Address (1931) the President stressed that
the continuation of the federal system required that all but
strictly national problems remain under the exclusive jurisdiction and responsibility of the states and their political
subdivisions. [16] Overlooked was the extraordinarily useful grant-in-aid mechanism which had been used successfully
before, and which met the demands both of states' rights
and of federal provision in issues of national concern.

Perhaps Hoover's most serious error was his failure to
understand the will of the American people. As Arthur
Ekirch writes,

> However justified the President's theories, they
> seemed out of touch with the political and social
> realities of the depression with its intense human
> problems and its multiplying examples of individual
> needs and suffering. [17]

All of Hoover's statements on the economic conditions of
the nation and all of his business forecasts could not take
the place of simple concern for the average man who was
frightened and hungry. As Frank Bane notes, the average
unemployed man does not have "any great overriding interest in the Gross National Product or whether prosperity
is just around the corner. What he needs is something which
will provide him with the wherewithal to take care of his
family Saturday night." [18] But this was hard for Herbert
Hoover to understand—not because he was without concern

—but rather because he was listening to the sound of a different drummer. [19]

"The fundamental business of the country, that is, production and distribution, is on a sound and prosperous basis." [20] These words of President Hoover, on the heels of the great stock market collapse of October 1929, proved to be wrong; however, the startling aspect of this remark is not the prediction, but the estimate of what constitutes the fundamental business of the nation. Hoover had become so bound by corporate interests that he placed their production and distribution above the interests of the average American. The fundamental business of the country was the health, welfare and security of its people—and if corporate production and distribution led to those goals, it should be supported—but always as a means, not as an end. This was what Herbert Hoover, the Great Humanitarian, tragically and indeed ironically had forgotten. "In the last analysis," writes historian Searle Charles, "Hoover the humanitarian was trapped by the Hoover who believed that 'the sole function of government is to bring about a condition of affairs favorable to the beneficial development of private enterprise.' " [21]   Such was the misfortune, both personal and national, that laid the setting for the election of 1932, and the advent of Roosevelt and Hopkins.

NOTES

1. The total number of workers in the country at that time was estimated to be about 35,000,000. See Senator Robert F. Wagner, Sr. testimony before the House Judiciary Committee in *Unemployment in the United States: Hearings,* 71st Congress, 2d Session (1930), p. 167.

2. Quoted in Harry L. Hopkins, *Spending to Save: The Complete Story of Relief* (New York: W. W. Norton, 1936), p. 24.

3. R. L. Wilbur and A. M. Hyde, *The Hoover Policies* (New

York: Charles Scribner's Sons, 1937), p. 375.

4. *Time*, XVIII (August 17, 1931), p. 7.

5. The figure of 5,500,000 unemployed by the end of 1930 is from Robert R. Nathan, *Estimates of Unemployment in the United States, 1929-1935* (Geneva: International Labor Organization, 1936). This report was prepared by Nathan for President Roosevelt's Committee on Economic Security. The figures are used because there are no official estimates of unemployment prepared under the Hoover Administration. Other organizations that prepared estimates were the National Industrial Conference Board, Alexander Hamilton Institute, National Research League and the American Federation of Labor.

6. For a detailed account of the activities of the Woods Committee, see E. P. Hayes, *Activities of the President's Emergency Committee for Employment* (Concord, Mass.: Rumford Press, 1936).

7. Irving Bernstein, *The Lean Years* (Boston: Houghton Mifflin, 1960), p. 460.

8. See Statement of Walter S. Gifford, *Hearings on Unemployment Relief* before a Subcommittee of the Committee on Manufacturers, U. S. Senate, 72d Cong., 1st Sess., on S. 174 and S. 262, December 29, 1931, p. 312.

9. *Ibid.*, p. 330; also see Bernstein, *Lean Years,* pp. 461-62.

10. Pub. L. 72-302, 72d Cong., 1st Sess., July 21, 1932.

11. Title II provided loans to the states and their political subdivisions for self-liquidating construction projects; Title III allotted funds for federal public works designated by Congress.

12. *New York Times,* October 23, 1932. Also see testimony of Treasury Secretary Ogden L. Mills, *Hearings,* Committee on Banking and Currency, U. S. Senate, 72d Cong., 1st Sess., S. 4755, June, 1932.

13. The following year Congress passed a bill rescinding the repayment provision, and thus the "loans" became outright grants, just as most political observers had expected.

14. See Brown, *Public Relief,* p. 127. In fairness, it should be noted that the RFC put executive direction of its administration of relief loans under an experienced social worker, Fred C. Croxton, who went considerably further than the bare letter of the law.

15. Wilbur and Hyde, *Hoover Policies,* p. 620.

16. For a clear statement to this effect see President Hoover's Lincoln's Day Address, February 12, 1931 in *Congressional Record,* 71st Cong., 3d Sess., LXXIV, Part V, p. 4835.

17. Arthur A. Ekirch, Jr., *Ideologies and Utopias: The Impact of the New Deal on American Thought* (Chicago: Quadrangle Books,

1969), p. 43.

18. Oral History Research Office, Columbia University, Bane MSS, p. 167.

19. Several books present a highly favorable reaction to President Hoover's handling of the crisis of this period. Myers and Newton, for example, cite Hoover for "offering federal leadership in mobilizing the economic resources . . . for meeting the problem of the depression." See W. S. Myers and W. H. Newton, *The Hoover Administration: A Documented Narrative* (New York: Charles Scribner's Sons, 1936); Wilbur and Hyde, *Hoover Policies;* and Theodore G. Joslin, *Hoover off the Record* (Garden City, N. Y.: Doubleday, Doran and Co., 1935).

20. Myers and Newton, *Hoover Administration, p. 23.*

21. Searle F. Charles, *Minister of Relief: Harry Hopkins and the Depression* (Syracuse, N. Y.: Syracuse University Press, 1963), p. 16.

3. Hopkins' Early Years: The Making of a Leader

In Retrospect

WHEN HARRY LLOYD HOPKINS died in 1946 at the age of 55, he had already done enough for his country to become something of a legend. His role during World War II in manpower mobilization, lend-lease planning, and service to Presidents Roosevelt and Truman as their personal envoy to Allied heads of state won the admiration of those who may have questioned his policies in federal relief administration. Moreover, as resident adviser and unofficial troubleshooter for President Roosevelt during the crucial opening years of the war, he served a function within our democratic system never quite duplicated—before or since.

Harry Hopkins was born in Sioux City, Iowa on August 17, 1890, one of five children of a harness maker and sometime travelling salesman. After having been wiped out in the depression of 1893, his father moved the family from town to town to establish themselves until they settled down in Grinnell, Iowa, which appealed to his mother because it was a college town. She was a fervent Methodist, and determined that her children would get a religious upbringing and a good education.

In 1912, Hopkins graduated from Grinnell College with

a bachelor's degree, Phi Beta Kappa key and an abundance of ambition. Convinced by one of his faculty friends to take a summer job with a boy's camp in New York State, he abandoned his youthful dream of publishing a newspaper in Montana and moved to New York City. After the summer, Hopkins joined the staff of the Association for Improving the Condition of the Poor, one of the largest and most influential private charitable agencies in the country. He started as a caseworker in its Bureau of Family Rehabilitation and Relief (at $40 a month), and served under the approving eye of the AICP director, John A. Kingsbury, until 1914. [1]

In 1914, John Purroy Mitchel was elected Mayor of New York City on a pledge to lead a reform administration. Mitchel called upon Kingsbury to serve as Commissioner of Public Charities. Kingsbury, in turn, brought Hopkins from the AICP to serve under him as executive secretary of the Board of Child Welfare. At age 25, Harry Hopkins entered the public service for the first time. He took full responsibility for administration of the new Mothers' Pension Law, established with a fund of $300,000 a year.

Rejected for military enlistment because of defective sight in one eye, Hopkins chose to serve during World War I with the Red Cross. Beginning in 1917 as director of their Gulf Division with headquarters in New Orleans, he soon was promoted to direct all Red Cross activities in the Southeastern states from a regional office in Atlanta. In the five years that Hopkins worked for the Red Cross in the South he developed a deep and lasting appreciation of the need for social work services in this often neglected section of the country. Later, when he directed the federal relief program, he gave special attention to the needs of the southern states for manpower and services.

In 1922 he returned to the AICP as director of its new

Health Division, but was lured away in 1924 to become executive director of the New York Tuberculosis Association. Under Hopkins' leadership, the Association expanded, absorbing the New York Heart Association, the Children's Welfare Federation and two major clinics, and changed its name to the New York Tuberculosis and Health Association. In the seven years he served there, Hopkins built the Association into one of the country's most powerful and successful research units in preventive medicine. [2]   In 1931, Governor Franklin D. Roosevelt invited this able administrator to Albany to direct the staff of his newly created Temporary Emergency Relief Administration (TERA).

His Personal Life

Mixed with the joys of his friendships and professional achievements was a life with more difficulties than one would expect the average man to face. Hopkins' main burden throughout his adult years was poor health, and he often joked that he thought of the Mayo Clinic as a second home. In his *New Yorker* profile of Hopkins, Geoffrey Hellman refers to him as looking "like an animated piece of shredded wheat," and, in view of Hopkins' digestive problem, it is no wonder. [3]   He suffered from stomach cancer in 1937, and a large part of his digestive system had to be removed, leaving him prey to various nutritional diseases that afflicted him repeatedly during the following years, and led to his premature death at 55 from inadequate digestive equipment, or hemochromatosis.

His home life was equally difficult. His first marriage ended in divorce, and his second wife, whom he adored, died of cancer after only seven years of marriage. Then in 1944 his youngest son, a Marine volunteer, was killed in

combat in the Pacific. [4]   Added to the weight of this
tragedy were his low salary and heavy expenses for medical
bills and alimony. When Hopkins came to Washington in
1933 he was earning only $10,000 as federal relief adminis-
trator which was $3,500 less than he received as director
of the New York Tuberculosis and Health Association
before entering government service. From this sum he had
to pay $6,000 a year in alimony, leaving precious little to
meet current expenses. [5]

However, Hopkins had a great ability to enjoy life, and
a remarkable capacity for making other people around
him cheerful, productive and glad to be with him. He
derived great pleasure from his work and the fellowship of
his colleagues, and it is said that he even found a genuine
amusement in being the frequent butt of political cartoons.
He was a positive, resilient man, and this was just the sort
of person Roosevelt wanted to have around during the
Depression. He enjoyed hard work, and people found
great pleasure in working for him. With the problems
Roosevelt faced, first in Albany and then in Washington,
Hopkins seemed just the blend of aggressive administrator
and loyal lieutenant any captain of state would want to
have on board.

The Task Begins

On August 25, 1931, Governor Franklin D. Roosevelt
called a special session of the New York State Legislature
and recommended that a Temporary Emergency Relief
Administration be established. A month later, after some
resistance from the Republican-controlled legislature, the
Wicks bill was passed and sent to the Governor for
signature. The Act provided for the establishment of the
Temporary Emergency Relief Administration comprised

of three members, serving without pay and by appointment of the Governor, and appropriated $20,000,000 for relief. The money was to be spent by the TERA for work relief during the winter months, either directly or through local governments. If work projects could not be developed in time, direct relief could be granted instead. New York thus became the first state to set up an emergency relief administration. [6]

As members of the TERA, Roosevelt appointed Philip Wickser, a Buffalo banker; John Sullivan, president of the State Federation of Labor; and Jesse Isidor Straus, president of R. H. Macy and Co., who was to serve as Chairman. Though these men proved devoted, they had limited time to spare; therefore the choice of an executive director was critical. Straus, on the advice of Lt. Gov. Herbert Lehman, offered the position to William Hodson, director of the Welfare Council in New York City. This move was appropriate, for it was Hodson who had urged Roosevelt to call the Legislature into special session to pass the Wicks Act legislation. But the Welfare Council would not release him, and Hodson declined. In doing so, he suggested that Roosevelt choose Harry L. Hopkins. [7]   Hopkins was promptly offered the position, accepted and, in typical fashion, began work the very next day. Hopkins served as executive director for a year and, after the resignation of Jesse Straus, was promoted to become TERA chairman.

The TERA Program

The TERA provided assistance to every tenth family in the State of New York. The original appropriation of $20 million had been intended to cover only the "emergency period" of November 1931 through May 1932, and was quickly exhausted. In addition, $5 million was allocated for the six months to follow and, simultaneously, the Legislature approved a bond issue of $30 million intended to cover the TERA program through the end of 1933. [8]

The task was huge, but under Hopkins' driving leadership, "TERA quickly became the outstanding relief organization in the nation and the model for other states and the federal government." [9]   The sums being granted were sparing, averaging about $23 a month per family, but in the acute deflation of the time, that was sufficient to keep families from starving. [10]   Some families at first hesitated to apply for relief when they could not find jobs or get assigned to a state work project. They felt home relief was charity which brought shame on the family. At Straus' insistence, Governor Roosevelt issued a public proclamation. It read, in part:

> I take this opportunity to urge all who have such hesitancy about applying for home relief to realize that home relief is in no sense charity. Home relief is being given to individuals to whom society will have failed in its obligations if it allows them to suffer through no fault of their own. [11]

In this one sentence, Roosevelt dashed the myth of self-reliance and asserted the responsibility of government to care for its citizens in time of depression. [12]   Relief was not a privilege, implied Roosevelt, but a right.

Plans for Federal Aid

After the presidential election of 1932, the President-elect and his staff began to think ahead to their forthcoming federal responsibilities. "I am more and more convinced," Hopkins wrote to Roosevelt that December, "that if we

are to meet the situation here in New York State through
1933, we are going to require assistance from the federal
government." [13]   Even relatively wealthy states like
New York could not continue to cope with the relief
burden through state bond issues. Based on his fourteen
months' experience with the TERA, Hopkins testified
before the United States Senate on the need for immediate
intervention on a scale and of a nature never before
effected. His testimony, in January 1933, was especially
significant, coming after the election of Roosevelt as
President, and less than two months before the inauguration. Hopkins outlined the principles of administration
and intergovernmental relations which took place under
the TERA, which, in large part, were made possible by the
granting of vast discretionary powers to Hopkins under the
Wicks Act. He strongly recommended that similar powers
be vested in a counterpart federal relief administrator in
the bill which was being discussed. Hopkins then underlined five major points: (1) All references to loans should
be stricken out of the bill; federal funds should be grants-
in-aid to the states; (2) the federal government should
deal directly (and exclusively) with the states; (3) the
federal funds should be in two parts, with approximately
half for reimbursement to the states, half as "free funds"
to be allotted at the discretion of the federal administrator
in cases where state funds appeared inadequate; (4) the
new federal administration should be established as a separate, independent agency, and not under the Reconstruction
Finance Corporation framework; and (5) that $600 million
to $1 billion should be appropriated. [14]   In submitting
an advance draft of this testimony to Roosevelt for comment, Hopkins added:

> You will note that this organization is very similar
> to the one you set up in the state, and it seems to

me it could work admirably in Washington. [15]

The New York State TERA program was important, therefore, not merely because it was the first emergency relief
administration in the nation, but because it served as a
prototype for the federal legislation which was to follow.
Its policies and procedures, its standards of relief and
personnel, and its imaginative administration were later
carried over into the national program when Roosevelt
became President, and Hopkins his administrator of relief.
For the Federal Emergency Relief Administration (FERA),
"though more complicated and far more important, was in
essence the extension of New York's TERA into the federal
government." [16]

NOTES

1. Hopkins was to serve under Dr. Kingsbury's supervision at
several points during his early career, and their association became
close, both personally and professionally. The influence of Kingsbury's leadership on Hopkins' development in these early years is
evident in the papers and correspondence, Kingsbury MSS, Library
of Congress.

2. Sherwood, *Roosevelt and Hopkins,* pp. 27-29.

3. Geoffrey T. Hellman, "Profile of Harry Hopkins," *The New
Yorker,* XIX (August 7, 1943).

4. Hopkins was first married in 1912 to Ethel Gross, and they
had three sons, Stephen, David and Robert. This marriage ended
seventeen years later in divorce. Hopkins married Barbara Duncan in
1929 and their brief, happy marriage ended with her death in 1937.
They had one daughter, Diana. Hopkins married Louise Macy in
1942, who survived him, and died in 1963.

5. At the insistence of social work friends, a "fund" of $5,000
a year was raised for two years to help Hopkins meet expenses.
Theoretically, this money was for lectures (which he rarely had time
to deliver). In January 1936, Hopkins' salary was increased by Congress to $12,000 and the subsidy from social work friends was ended.

Hopkins continued to receive frequent honorariums for speeches and articles, and some of these were substantial. Frank Bane indicates that Hopkins received $1,000 for an annual speech to the American Public Welfare Association (interview, April 21, 1970); and records show, for example, that Hopkins received $5,000 for one article in *The American Magazine* (Personal Correspondence File, Hopkins MSS, Hyde Park Collection).

6. Many more state relief programs were established in 1932, and by the summer of 1933, state organizations were functioning in every state except Wyoming. See Williams, *Federal Aid,* p. 19.

7. Hopkins thus entered Roosevelt's service without Roosevelt's participating in any way in the selection process or even having seen him except for a casual handshake during the 1928 campaign. Franklin D. Roosevelt as Governor MSS, Hyde Park Collection; Letter, Chairman Straus to Lt. Gov. Lehman, October 7, 1931.

8. The $30 million dollar bond issue was approved at a voter referendum in November 1932 by four-to-one; a second bond issue of $60 million dollars was approved in November 1933. Thus New York State made $115 million available for relief. See Emma O. Lundberg, "The New York State Temporary Emergency Relief Administration," *Social Service Review,* VI (December 1932), pp. 545-66.

9. Bernstein, *Lean Years,* p. 458. Later Lorena A. Hickok, Hopkins' Chief Field Investigator for FERA, noted after a week's tour of New York State, "I found relief administration so far ahead of what I had seen in other states that there just isn't any basis for comparison at all. New York State's Temporary Emergency Relief Administration has just about achieved . . . it seems to me, what the Federal Emergency Relief Administration is aiming at for the rest of the country." (Report for Week of September 12-19, 1933, Hickok File, Hopkins MSS, Hyde Park Collection.)

10. New York's relief program was munificent compared with some in other areas of the country. In Southern Illinois, for example, the Red Cross was able to give families of coal miners only $3 for food per month; and relief payments in Detroit dropped to five cents per day per person.

11. Enclosure to Letter, Chairman Straus to Governor Roosevelt, January 5, 1932, Franklin D. Roosevelt as Governor MSS, Hyde Park Collection.

12. For a detailed account of the work of the New York State TERA during the Depression, see Alexander L. Radomski, *Work*

Relief in New York State: 1931-1935 (New York: King's Crown Press, 1947); Bernard Bellush, *Franklin D. Roosevelt as Governor of New York* (New York: Columbia University Press, 1955), Ch. 7; and *Five Million People, One Billion Dollars* (Albany, N. Y.: Temporary Emergency Relief Administration, 1937).

13. Letter, TERA Chairman Hopkins to Governor Roosevelt, December 14, 1932, Franklin D. Roosevelt as Governor MSS, Hyde Park Collection.

14. See Hearings on Senate 5125, January 1933 in Brown, *Public Relief,* pp. 79-86; and enclosure to letter, TERA Chairman Hopkins to Governor Roosevelt, December 14, 1932.

15. Letter, TERA Chairman Hopkins to Governor Roosevelt, December 14, 1932.

16. Grace K. Adams, *Workers on Relief* (New Haven, Conn.: Yale University Press, 1939), p. 9.

Part II

HOPKINS
TAKES COMMAND

Ickes is a good administrator but often too
slow. Harry gets things done. I am going to
give this job to Harry.

Franklin D. Roosevelt

When a house is on fire you don't call a
conference; you put it out!

Harry L. Hopkins

4. The FERA: Uncle Sam Assumes Responsibility

Roosevelt Responds

ON May 12, 1933, two months after his inauguration, President Franklin D. Roosevelt approved the Federal Emergency Relief Act of 1933, appropriating $500,000,000 to aid the states in meeting their immediate relief needs. To implement this program, the Act established the Federal Emergency Relief Administration (FERA), which officially came into existence on May 22, 1933—just ten days after the President signed the bill. Of the initial half billion dollars, $250,000,000 was to be made available to the states on a matching basis of one to three. The other $250,000,000 was to form a discretionary fund from which sums could be granted to those states whose relief needs exceeded their ability to meet the matching provisions. Indeed, it was just as Harry Hopkins had recommended.

President Roosevelt's first choice for FERA administrator was his able TERA chairman, but Herbert Lehman, who was now Governor of New York, objected strongly. While Lehman insisted that Hopkins could not be spared from his post in Albany, Hopkins made it clear that one does not say "no" to the President of the United States, and on May 22, 1933, was sworn in at the White House to

his new federal post. Hopkins then took a taxi to his
shabby office in the old Walker-Johnson Building and set
up a desk on the top floor in the hallway. He promptly
notified the forty-eight governors to form state relief
organizations, and by nightfall had made the initial FERA
grants to seven states for just over $5 million. [1]   By the
end of June, grants had been made to forty-five states, the
District of Columbia and the Territory of Hawaii, amounting to approximately $51,000,000. Thus, in a little more
than a month, Hopkins already had disbursed twice as
much money as federal relief administrator as he had in his
year and a half with the TERA. [2]

The FERA program operated in two phases, the first
(1933-34) running prior to, and then simultaneously with
the Civil Works Administration; the second (1934-35)
starting at the close of the Civil Works Administration
(CWA) program in the spring of 1934, and ending when
emergency relief gave way to the Works Progress Administration (WPA). During the first phase, the FERA
primarily gave direct relief; the work relief it offered had
little emphasis on quality control, was hastily planned and,
by Roosevelt's own admission, often of the "leaf-raking"
variety. [3] During the winter of 1933-34, while the CWA
was still operating, the FERA continued to function
chiefly in supervising a direct relief program for unemployables, and in developing special programs for farmers,
teachers and transients.

The second phase of the FERA was known as the Emergency Work Program. It picked up many of the employables who had been with the CWA during the winter, and
continued those projects which had not been completed.
The emphasis was on public construction, and when it
came to a halt in the summer of 1935, more than 240,000
projects had been completed. "The shift from the dole to
work relief proceeded so far in the later phases of the

FERA," one observer concluded, "that in 1935, during the last months of its existence, the agency counted nearly half of its beneficiaries as workers." [4]

The Grant-in-Aid Mechanism

In operating the FERA program, Roosevelt and Hopkins decided to reject the notion of a totally federal program and opt for a state and local partnership under the grant-in-aid system. There were several reasons for their decision. First, they did not have time to start from scratch in building their own relief organization. The crisis of unemployment and destitution would not wait for an elaborate structure to be built, and it was not Roosevelt's style to delay action under such conditions. By 1933, almost every state in the union had its own emergency relief program; hence it would be only logical to work through the existing framework. Second, federalization of the relief effort would have been highly unpopular politically and surely would have met considerable opposition in Congress. Firm in their belief in states' rights and in their preference for localism, legislators certainly would have claimed that an entirely federal program infringed upon state sovereignty and American tradition. Third, many leaders viewed emergency relief as "temporary"—a short-term measure to lift the country out of a crisis. They were not sure how long the Depression would last, and therefore were reluctant to build a vast, expensive and new federal structure. Finally, the alternative, as adopted, would rely on the grant-in-aid system, a familiar and accepted pattern of intergovernmental relations. First embodied in the Morrill Act of 1862 (and supplementary legislation), the practice had grown increasingly common in the 20th century. By the pre-Depression years of the late 1920s, federal grants-in-aid to the states each year were averaging $140,000,000, of which nearly 60 percent was for highway construction. [5] In short, the grant-in-aid principle would be politically acceptable. relatively quick to apply and easy to administer, and permit adequate federal controls over what would be an essentially state and local program. [6]

The Question of Control

Hopkins did not rely solely upon rules and regulations to achieve his objectives but implemented regulations with other control devices designed to assure substantial compliance with federal policies. They were the familiar control devices inherent in the grant-in-aid system: prior FERA approval of all state relief plans and programs; insistence upon the appointment and retention of qualified personnel in both state and local relief organizations; and a system of regular, detailed state reports concerning the nature of the relief program and the expenditure of funds. Hopkins then supplemented these formal procedures with field reports from his own network of federal regional offices, and by on-site inspections made by his roving staff of investigators. [7]

In addition, Hopkins had an ultimate weapon. Section 3(b) of the Federal Emergency Relief Act stated:

> The Administrator may, under rules and regulations prescribed by the President, assume control of the administration in any State or States where, in his judgment, more effective and efficient cooperation between the State and Federal authorities may thereby be secured in carrying out the purposes of this Act. [8]

Although this power was invoked in only six states during the life of the FERA, it set an important precedent in the field of public administration. [9] The power which was given by Congress to the Administration for assuming control of the administration of federal funds in a state constituted, in effect, a recognition by both the legislative and executive branches that the citizens of this country are federal citizens and have rights which transcend state lines and the jurisdiction of state governments. [10]

The Administration of Public Funds

Hopkins and the FERA established a series of important precedents, of which virtually every one proved to be controversial. The Administrator's first confrontation was with the voluntary social work sector which saw itself as the logical recipient of much of the new public funding. After all, the voluntary agencies already had a core staff with years of training and experience. They were known and accepted in their communities and had a reputation for fiscal integrity.

Without denying any of these claims, Hopkins used his broad powers under the FERA legislation to assert that these new federal monies would remain under public control. In his first regular memorandum to the states on June 23, 1933, Hopkins was explicit:

> Grants of Federal emergency relief funds are to be administered by public agencies...This ruling prohibits the turning over of Federal Emergency Relief funds to a private agency. The unemployed must apply to a public agency for relief, and this relief must be furnished direct to the applicant by a public agent. [11]

"This policy was epoch-making," notes Josephine C. Brown, "in that it established once and for all a clean-cut principle and a broad philosophy of governmental responsibility for relief." [12]   Public money, Hopkins implied, was a public trust, and should be under the auspices and control of the public sector. [13]

The debate then began on the question of how the relief should be given. Hopkins' two advisers, Frank Bane (from public welfare) and C.M. Bookman (from the voluntary field), differed sharply in their recommendations. Bane felt Hopkins should experiment with cash payments, while Bookman held to the tradition of giving relief "in kind," i.e., with commissary food, grocery orders, or coupons redeemable at a warehouse for clothing. Precedent clearly was in Bookman's favor. Even under the TERA in New York State, perhaps the most pioneering in pre-1933 relief legislation, only work relief could be paid in cash. Direct (home) relief had to be paid "in kind" by terms of the statute.

Hopkins decided to break with past practice and offer cash relief in all cases. In inviting states and localities to join him in this experiment, he specified that

> relief shall be in the form of food, shelter, clothing, light, fuel, necessary household supplies, medicine, medical supplies, and medical attendance, *or the cash equivalent of these to the person in his home...* [14]

While the response from state and local government administrations was slow and cautious, a trend toward experimentation with cash relief tended to grow in late 1934 and early 1935. [15]   With the option for giving cash established, Hopkins had turned an important corner in the history of home relief in this country, and a pattern for the future had been firmly suggested, not only for relief

but for the categorical programs in the Social Security Act
of 1935 as well.

Work Test versus Work Relief

Hopkins insisted that under the FERA, work relief be substituted for the work test. The work test, a product of the
Elizabethan Poor Law, required the relief recipient to perform some hard, disagreeable form of manual labor—such
as work in the woodpile—in order to receive any "outdoor
relief" whatsoever. There were no regular hours, nor any
attempt to simulate useful employment. The idea was to
make the work sufficiently unpleasant to dissuade all but
the most desperate and needy from applying.

Work relief springs from an entirely different social
philosophy. Its goal is meaningful and nonpunitive forms
of work to maintain the morale, skills and pride of employ-
able persons forced to accept relief. It is based on the
premise that needy workers may be jobless through no
cause of their own making and are entitled to aid from
their government. In defending work relief from its critics,
Hopkins wrote:

> For a long time those who did not require relief
> entertained the illusion that those being aided were
> in need through some fault of their own. It is now
> pretty clear in the national mind that the unem-
> ployed are a cross-section of the workers, the finest
> people in the land. [16]

In making clear that people on relief "were like anyone
else," Hopkins helped to remove some of the stigma from
"being on relief." While he was not entirely successful because of the limitations of the FERA program, his public

declarations along with his abolition of the work-test philosophy were important factors in helping people begin to
view public relief as an indisputable right instead of a
privilege.

White-Collar Projects

In his campaign for increasing public respect for the relief
recipient, Hopkins stressed self-determination. A person on
work relief, he argued, should be able to choose a job closely
related to his ordinary occupation and interests. While this
philosophy was not controversial in theory, it became the
subject of heated debate when translated into white-collar
projects. In the mind of many Americans—still under the
influence of the poor laws and the work test—work involved
physical labor. Hopkins fought back. In response to a
reporter's question on the value and propriety of painting
murals, making new dictionaries and conducting social
science research, Hopkins confronted his attackers:

> ...There is nothing wrong with that. They are damn
> good projects—excellent projects...These fellows can
> make fun and shoot at white-collar people, if they
> want to. I notice somebody says facetiously, repair
> all streets. That is all they think about...money to
> repair streets. I think there are things in life besides
> that...We don't need any apologies. [17]

He believed that if it were preferable to have an unemployed
bricklayer work on a construction project, a violin player
should earn his relief money with a symphony orchestra
and not by trying to lay sewer pipes. [18] He successfully
checked the tide of criticism, and in doing so, helped to
turn the mind of Americans away from Poor Law thinking

toward a more democratic concept of public relief.

In the Context of History

Toward the end of the 1930s, when Samuel Rosenman was collecting Roosevelt's public papers for publication, he asked the President to comment on some of the most important pieces of legislation. In reflecting upon the FERA, Roosevelt felt it was expressive of a new government attitude toward relief in three ways.

First, "it recognized that relief was a social problem to be administered by a social agency rather than by the Reconstruction Finance Corporation (RFC), which was purely a financial agency." The emergency relief administrations functioned as social agencies throughout the country, and in Washington, Hopkins gave the program a distinctly social orientation. The FERA was not a financial operation to rescue business but a social program to rescue lives.

Second, Roosevelt noted, FERA "provided for outright grants to States for relief" rather than making loans repayable with interest. In this sense, the federal legislation recognized the superior fiscal resources of the national government and committed itself to a grant of funds that would not have to be repaid.

Finally, and most important, the new statute "recognized that relief was not the complete responsibility of the States and their local political subdivisions," and that the federal government shared responsibility for meeting the problem. [19]   In effect, the federal government was becoming a partner in the business of relief.

Both Roosevelt and Hopkins stressed that the emergency relief effort would be a partnership, and that the states and localities would have to continue to use all of their

bonding and taxing powers to provide their fair share of
the financial burden. As Hopkins noted,

> In some instances, State authorities...have taken
> an attitude in complete reversal to that assumed
> by Congress in passing the [FERA] Act. These
> authorities have assumed that it was the obligation
> of the federal government to bear all or substan-
> tially all of the relief burden and accordingly, have
> resented insistence by the Relief Administration
> that their States contribute a fair proportion of
> relief expenses... [20]

A partnership, he stressed, meant both partners had to
share administrative as well as fiscal responsibility. [21]

The Task Fulfilled

Following the creation of the WPA in May 1935, the
FERA gradually was brought to a close, and it was prac-
tically terminated on June 30. A small cadre remained for
six more months to supervise the formal transition of the
program, after which no new projects were initiated. The
FERA was continued legally until June 30, 1938 in order
to fulfill commitments and discharge its outstanding
obligations. [22]

There is dispute as to how much the FERA accomplished, and whether it marked the start of modern public
welfare in America, or whether this came only with the
WPA and social security legislation. "If our present immense and varied welfare programs had their origins in the
1930s," writes Raymond Moley, "the date must be 1935
rather than 1933." [23] But this would appear only par-
tially true, for the FERA revolutionized the system of

public relief which had gone virtually unchanged for more
than three hundred years. In doing so, it pioneered with
such innovations as federal assistance to the poor, direct
cash relief, work relief, public social services and the use
of grants-in-aid to states as an administrative tool for federal assistance to the poor. Our "immense and varied welfare programs" of today surely were built, in part, on the
foundations which such FERA innovations provided, for
they are accepted principles in public welfare today.

Moreover, the FERA stands out as one of the most important expressions of a new concept of government which
calls for federal action in the interest of human welfare
under a complex economic system over which the individual has small control. It brought on, in effect, a new and
social interpretation of the "welfare clause" in the Constitution which had served to restrict federal relief policy
since President Pierce's veto of proposed welfare legislation
in 1854. [24]

NOTES

1. Colorado, Illinois, Iowa, Michigan, Mississippi, Ohio and
Texas.

2. By the end of December approximately $324,500,000 had
been allocated to forty-eight states and all the Territories to which
the Act applied. Under five different Acts of Congress, the FERA
was provided with just over $3 billion. See Brown, *Public Relief*,
p. 148.

3. This defect in the early work relief program was due partly
to the FERA rule that federal funds could not be used for the purchase of materials, a fact which handicapped the development of
worthwhile projects until it was corrected in 1934. See Samuel I.
Rosenman, ed., *The Public Papers and Addresses of Franklin D.
Roosevelt* (New York: Random House, 1938), II, p. 242.

4. Dixon Wecter, *Age of the Great Depression* (New York:
Macmillan Co., 1948), p. 74. For a detailed account of the emergency

work relief phase, see "The Emergency Work Relief Program of the FERA: April 1, 1934–July 1, 1935," FERA File, Current Series, National Archives.

5. Austin F. Macdonald, *Federal Aid* (New York: Thomas Y. Crowell Co., 1928), p. 6. Also see V. O. Key, Jr., *The Administration of Federal Grants to States* (Chicago: Public Administration Service, 1937).

6. Under the FERA, for the first time all three levels of government (federal, state and local) were involved in the administration of relief. But the bulk of the work of administering relief rested with the local governments and local relief officials. Contrary to popular misconception, the federal government did not directly administer relief in the localities. It respected the rights of state and local governments, while supplying close to 71 percent of the funds.

7. Each of the regional offices had a research adviser responsible for collecting statistical data from the respective states. This information then was consolidated monthly by the FERA Division of Research and Statistice to provide the Administration with a uniform set of nationwide relief statistics.

8. Federal Emergency Relief Act of 1933, Pub. L. 73-15, 73d Congress.

9. Relief was federalized in Oklahoma on February 23, 1934; North Dakota on March 1, 1934; Massachusetts on March 7, 1934; Ohio on March 16, 1935; Louisiana on April 8, 1935; and Georgia on April 19, 1935.

10. Brown, *Public Relief,* p. 208.

11. Federal Emergency Relief Administration, *Rules and Regulations No. 1,* June 23, 1933, Section I, Hopkins MSS, Hyde Park Collection. Thereafter, all federal relief funds were distributed to clients through public agencies, except in Chicago, where Roman Catholic charity organizations were funded for a considerable period of time, despite FERA regulations.

12. Brown, *Public Relief,* p. 186.

13. Interview with Frank Bane, April 21, 1970.

14. Federal Emergency Relief Administration, *Rules and Regulations, No. 3,* July 11, 1933. (Italics added.)

15. The FERA *Monthly Report* for March 1935 showed that at the end of 1934, three-fourths of all direct relief still was being paid in kind, but noted, "there is definite evidence of a tendency toward payment of direct relief in cash." While in May 1934, only six states were paying as much as 25 percent of the total direct relief in

cash, fourteen states were in this category by December. See Colcord, *Cash Relief*, p. 42.

16. Quoted in Robert P. Post, "Grappling the Vast Problem of Relief," *New York Times Magazine*, July 8, 1934.

17. Press Conference, April 6, 1935, Hopkins MSS, Hyde Park Collection.

18. Harry L. Hopkins, "Boondoggling: It Is a Social Asset," *Christian Science Monitor*, August 19, 1936, Magazine section.

19. Rosenman, *Public Papers*, II, p. 184.

20. *Expenditure of Funds*, FERA, Senate Document No. 86, 74th Cong., 1st Sess., p. xix.

21. The total amount of obligations incurred for the three-year life of the FERA was just over $4 billion of which approximately $3 billion (71 percent) was federal. During the first quarter of 1935, when the relief load was at its peak, 77.8 percent of the funds were federal, 9.6 percent state and 12.6 percent local. See Williams, *Federal Aid*, pp. 83-85.

22. For a detailed account of the work of the FERA see Doris Carothers, *Chronology of the Federal Emergency Relief Administration*, FERA Research Monograph VI (Washington: U.S. Government Printing Office, 1937); Brown, *Public Relief*; and Williams, *Federal Aid*.

23. Raymond Moley, *The First New Deal* (New York: Harcourt, Brace and World, 1966), p. 282.

24. In his message to Congress on June 8, 1934, Roosevelt said: "If, as our Constitution tells us, our federal government was established among other things 'to promote the general welfare,' it is our plain duty to provide for that security upon which welfare depends." Rosenman, *Public Papers*, III, p. 291.

5. Civil Works: The Winter of '33

Putting Men to Work

ON OCTOBER 30, 1933, Harry Hopkins met with the President to discuss a plan he and his staff had worked out to put men to work for the winter. It was an ambitious and expensive plan, but they thought they could try it out on the Chief Executive. "We thought this was going to be a preliminary presentation to the President," recalls Frank Bane. "It was something he would think about and probably decide in a couple of weeks. Harry came back flabbergasted and said not only had the President bought it lock, stock and barrel, but he had provided the money!" [1]

The Civil Works Administration (CWA) was created just nine days later by Executive Order under Title II of the National Industrial Recovery Act with Harry Hopkins serving as Administrator concurrently with his parallel post at the FERA. The program started six days later, and on November 22, 1933 payroll checks were issued for the first week's work to 814,511 workers in a total amount of more than $7,500,000. [2] Typically, Hopkins had lost no time in translating an idea into action.

The CWA was fundamentally different from the FERA in several ways. First, CWA was an entirely federal program,

not a grant-in-aid style cooperative venture. Second, it was
to be temporary—perhaps for three or four months—just to
cover the winter. Third, it was exclusively a work program
paying a cash wage at a prevailing rate determined by category of work and region. The goal was publicly stated at
the outset: to put 4,000,000 persons to work for the
winter.

The Need for Such a Program

The decision to start a new, short-term works program was
not as undecipherable as it might seem. Harold Ickes' Public Works Administration (PWA) had been slow in getting
started and the economy was suffering. Why not promote
recovery through the injection of purchasing power into
the economy—adrenalin-style? Such a stimulant Hopkins
believed might prime the pump in big cities and small towns
throughout the nation. Second, it could serve as a labora-
tory for experimentation with a federal work program. As
Searle Charles suggests, it could be a "trial balloon" which
would set precedents for switching later from emergency relief to a full-scale program of meaningful public work. [3]
   Most important of all, however, Civil Works was designed for very human reasons: to give men an opportunity to *work* for money, rather than stand in line for it.
In this sense, the plan typified Hopkins, concerned first
and foremost with people and their common human need
for dignity, wages and warmth for the winter. "As a social
worker," notes one observer, "he was noted for putting
human needs ahead of achievements in steel and concrete." [4]   While long-range plans to build up industry
were fine, his first concern was in redirecting the energies
of the nation from business to people—from stimulating
production, to stimulating the minds and muscle of men.

The Task of Implementation

To achieve these goals, the CWA initiated small, federally sponsored work projects across the nation. Because they had to lend themselves to a quick start and rapid completion, the projects did not involve major construction. Despite the importance of the CWA white-collar program, approximately 90 percent of the CWA projects were those involving manual labor such as road construction and repair, maintenance of parks and playgrounds, pest control and soil conservation. These were the sort of tasks that needed to be done and, unlike the building of large highways, dams and bridges, could be completed quickly.

The program was extremely popular with state and local officials because 90 percent of the funds came from the Federal Treasury. In this sense it was an extravagant program, costing the federal government $833,960,000 for four and one-half months of operation. Almost 80 percent of this money, however, went directly into men's pockets as wages. [5] To finance Civil Works, Roosevelt simply transferred $400,000,000 from Ickes' PWA program to Hopkins' new works operation, and while this did not sit well with "curmudgeon" Ickes, Hopkins was secretly delighted. Hopkins then added on some $89,960,000 from unused FERA funds and pressured Congress for a supplemental appropriation of $345,000,000 when the program's political popularity had been firmly established later that winter. Said Hopkins:

> ...unemployed people simply want to work for what they get. They resent being asked to be a party to any subterfuge of a job as a means of getting relief. And for my part, I glory in their refusal and resentment of all such subterfuges. [6]

Apparently, Hopkins was right. This was what the people wanted, and when you had the right idea, it was not hard to get money for it.

The Task Accomplished

Just two months after the CWA began operations, it reached its goal of putting 4,000,000 Americans back to work. It was a phenomenal achievement. [7]   In one winter Hopkins and his central staff of 121 people had mobilized almost as many men as had served in the armed forces during World War I. "Well, they're at work," Hopkins is said to have reported to Roosevelt, "but for God's sake, don't ask me what they're doing." [8]

Tributes came from all over. As Rexford Tugwell remarked, "The ingenuity and courage with which the task of providing employment was undertaken by Hopkins and his group startled the whole country." [9] "I wonder if you have any idea of what CWA is doing for the morale of these people and the communities," wrote Lorena Hickok from a field inspection in Iowa. "Officials, like the mayor of Sioux City, tell me it's almost beyond belief. And they wouldn't need to tell me. I can see it for myself." [10]

As Edward A. Williams remarks,

> From the point of view of intergovernmental relations, it [CWA] stands out as the most amazing example of federal and state-local cooperation ever witnessed in this country. Only in time of war has this nation ever experienced the will to action, the federal-state cooperation, and the cutting of red tape which prevailed throughout the C.W.A. era [11]

To this, a New Deal historian adds, "the CWA stands out in all American history as one of the greatest peacetime administrative feats ever completed. For this Hopkins and his staff must be given credit." [12]   And one Senator remarked profanely, with both respect and indignation: "If Roosevelt ever becomes Jesus Christ, he should have Harry Hopkins as his prophet." [13]

Important Innovations

In setting up the CWA, Hopkins deliberately designed it so that both those who had been receiving direct relief and those who had not chosen to do so would be accepted and work side-by-side in relatively equal numbers. Only half the men, therefore, were taken from the relief rolls; the other half could simply apply directly for work and were to be asked for no proof of need. They were not to be investigated or submitted to a "means test."

Hopkins was above all a social worker, and he understood that if the program were to be successful in rehabilitating men, in body and mind, it must strive to be without stigma. His solution was bold with experimentation. The CWA would not just be for those who got the dole, but for all those who needed a job, regardless of their previous condition. In large measure, the stigmatizing means test was avoided, and workers could proudly say, "I'm working for the government."

Hopkins was equally insistent that the "budgetary deficit" principle used for payment in the FERA be replaced in the CWA by a regular wage. Under the former system, within state and local regulations, social workers in the local relief agency set the maximum amount to be allowed a given family on the basis of prepared family budgets. Then the income of the family, if any, was determined.

The relief agency supplied the budgetary deficiency—the difference between the amount estimated to be required and the family income. In other words, the money earned on the FERA work relief jobs was really an "allowance," equal to the difference between the total budget needs of the family and any other income which they might be able to count on. Again, Hopkins understood that the difference between an "allowance" and a "wage" had trementous psychological significance for the recipient who preferred the dignity associated with the latter. The CWA therefore became the first government program of public relief to pay cash to workers at a prevailing wage.

As the CWA program came to a close in March 1934, it was clear that it had made quite an impact on the nation and had set the stage for the expanded and more permanent work program which was to follow. [14]

NOTES

1. "The President then called in the press," Bane recalls, "and told them...'We'll have this in operation in thirty days.' " Oral History Research Office, Columbia University, Bane MSS, p. 169.

2. Rosenman, *Public Papers,* II, p. 458.

3. Charles, *Minister of Relief,* Ch. III. Hopkins later wrote, "without what they learned through the CWA experience they never could have launched WPA, and to that extent it can be looked upon as a preliminary, almost a probationary period." Hopkins, *Spending to Save,* p. 124.

4. Bernard Asbell, *The F.D.R. Memoirs* (New York: Doubleday and Company, 1973), p. 194.

5. The worker averaged $15.04 a week under the CWA; only $6.50 a week under the FERA program.

6. Harry L. Hopkins, "The War on Distress," *Today,* I (December 16, 1933), p. 9.

7. Employment reached its peak during the week ending January 18, 1934 with 4,263,644 CWA workers earning more than $64,000,000 per week. See Rosenman, *Public Papers,* II, p. 458.

8. Marquis Childs, "The President's Best Friend," *Saturday Evening Post* (April 19, 1941), p. 11.

9. Rexford G. Tugwell, *The Democratic Roosevelt* (Garden City, N.Y.: Doubleday and Co., 1957), p. 320.

10. Letter, Lorena Hickok to Harry Hopkins, November 25, 1933, Hickok File, Hopkins MSS, Hyde Park Collection.

11. Williams, *Federal Aid,* p. 123.

12. Charles, *Minister of Relief,* p. 65.

13. *Time,* February 19, 1934.

14. For a detailed account of the work of CWA see Colcord, *Cash Relief;* A.W. Macmahon, J.D. Millett and Gladys Ogden, *The Administration of Federal Work Relief (*Chicago: Public Administration Service, 1941); and Williams, *Federal Aid.*

6. The WPA—Mighty Oak

The Germination of an Idea

WHEN THE CWA came to a close in the spring of 1934, the country returned to emergency relief. By the fall, FERA listed 18,323,000 persons as relief recipients, but millions of men who had tasted the dignity of work that winter again wanted jobs. These men simply wanted to get off relief and back into the productive mainstream of American life.

Hopkins evaluated the situation. There was no reason, he thought,

> why these unemployed people should be asked to live as exiles in their own country, finding courage only in the hope that some day they may be admitted to the magic circle. Either a way must be found to admit them to participation in the economy of private enterprise or else they must be given a definite and respectable status as recipients of insurance benefits or as public workers. [1]

In other words, Hopkins was becoming convinced that more had to be done for a greater number of people than under the emergency relief program of the FERA. Men were hungry not only for food, but for the jobs and self-respect they had known for those fleeting months under the Civil Works Administration. Hopkins summed up his reflections in his book, *Spending to Save:*

> In addition to want, the unemployed were confronting a still further destructive force, that of worklessness. They were accustomed to making a return for their livelihood. It was a habit they liked, and from which they chiefly drew their self-respect.

> We can talk all we want to about some coming civilization in which work will be outmoded, and in which we shall enjoy a state of being rather than one of action, but contemporary sentiment is still against "a man who gets something for nothing." [2]

Hopkins' goal was for a massive program of public works with responsibility for the unemployables returned to the states. After the Democrats' sweeping victory in the congressional elections of 1934, he knew that it was time to begin work on a plan. Hopkins turned to his key staff members as soon as the election returns were in and said,

> Boys, this is our hour. We've got to get everything we want—a works program, social security, wages and hours, everything—now or never. Get your minds to work on developing a complete ticket to provide security for all the folks of this country up and down and across the board. [3]

They retired for days of intensive planning and by Thanksgiving a program was ready to be presented to the President.

The Plan and Roosevelt's Reaction

The plan drafted by Hopkins and his aides essentially was simple, based on their commitment to a works program and the success of the CWA experience. The goal would be to replace relief with a permanent program of public work, strengthened in scope and substance by adaptation of some of the rigorous PWA standards. The federal government would provide jobs for as long as they were needed to the unemployed on the relief rolls, and turn back to local authorities responsibility for the unemployables. [4]

Hopkins knew that Roosevelt would have to make a political decision: should the Administration continue its attempt to secure and maintain support among industrial leaders, or should it launch, in effect, a "Second New Deal" of recovery *and* reform which would move the country decisively to the left? With the substantial vote of confidence at the polls very much in mind, Roosevelt decided that the position of the conservatives and Liberty Leaguers was weakened. The plan seemed politically feasible and ideologically sound. He told Hopkins to get all the details down on paper and ready for Congress by the New Year.

A Tree is Planted

In his annual message to Congress on January 4, 1935, Roosevelt presented the new plan to the nation. The FERA would be superseded by a coordinated program of emergency public employment for the 3-1/2 million able-bodied persons on the relief rolls. This would be a federal program of useful public projects united under a single, new and greatly expanded administration. For those who were unemployable—then amounting to 1-1/2 million on the FERA rolls—the states and localities would reassume responsibility, but with a new program of categorical assistance that would provide federal grants-in-aid for many.

Roosevelt was proposing to divide up the FERA's 5 million cases into two portions. His reasoning went thus: first, since the unemployable needy had been cared for by the states and their localities before the Depression, in the future they should be cared for as before; the President thereby reaffirmed the traditional principle of local responsibility for these persons, although now there would be the prospect of federal financial assistance for certain categories of the dependent under the proposed social security legislation. Second, the problem regarding the employables was different and the response must be different. This group was the victim of a nationwide Depression caused by conditions which were not local but national; hence, the primary responsibility for alleviating unemployment lay with the federal government which must create a large-scale work program for those on relief who want jobs. [5]

The legislation was drafted, and on April 8, 1935, the Emergency Relief Appropriation Act of 1935 was passed by the Congress. It had been just five months since Hopkins and his staff sat down to map their new plan "to provide security for all the folks of this country." It would not be quite so perfect or nearly so simple, but it would be a landmark for the nation.

The Overall Program

The new federal works agency was composed of three operational divisions. First, there was a Division of Applications and Information to receive all suggested plans (federal, state or local), sort and check them, and then pass

them on to the Advisory Committee on Allotments. This
Committee would study the proposals and recommend
their acceptance or rejection to the President. Finally, the
Works Progress Division (soon changed to "Administration") would have the apparently minor role of investigating, regulating and reporting. For example, it would
check that man-year costs were right, that men were available for the project, and that the different federal work
projects meshed with each other. [6]

However, in the Executive Order establishing the Works
Progress Administration (WPA) there was one seemingly
insignificant paragraph tucked away at the end:

> In addition to the foregoing powers and duties the
> Works Progress Administration shall... recommend
> and carry on small useful projects designed to assure
> a maximum of employment in all localities. [7]

Although oblique and seemingly little more than an after-
thought, this provision proved to be just the loophole that
its Administrator, Harry Hopkins, needed. Those "small
useful projects" eventually represented an expenditure of
more than $10 billion.

While the emphasis in the Emergency Relief Appropriations Act of April 8, and the Executive Order of May 6,
clearly was on the WPA as an instrument of monitoring,
coordination and service, one cannot believe that Roosevelt was entirely naïve in his visions for Hopkins. In light of
the works program's main goal—the rapid employment of
3½ million employables from the relief rolls with a $4
billion fund appropriated by Congress—the dominance of
the WPA (and Hopkins) would have seemed almost inevitable.

First, at an average man-year cost that divides out to
$1,142 (i.e., $4 billion ÷ 3.5 million persons)—all cost of

materials and administration *as well as* payrolls included—
it is clear that the great PWA schemes for public construction were out of the question. Ickes' PWA projects
would demand too great an outlay for purchase of materials
and land to leave adequate money out of this meager allotment for wages. [8] Second, Roosevelt indicated explicitly,
when he sent his works program to Congress, that he wanted to reach his goal of putting the 3½ million employables
to work promptly—indeed, within a year if not less. The
PWA was not geared to work so swiftly. Public building
construction, rehousing, and building bridges and dams
took long periods of time for technical training, land ac-
quisition and engineer planning. While such projects held
significant long-range value for the economy and the physical plant of the country, clearly they were not well suited
to the immediate goals which the President had in mind. [9]

Therefore, in retrospect, it would seem that Roosevelt
must have been aware that Hopkins' WPA would be playing
a leading role in the works program. Given the goals the
President set himself, it could not have worked any other
way. By the end of 1935, the WPA had been allocated over
one billion dollars—by far the largest allotment to any
agency—and was well on its way to a dominant position
in the new works program.

The WPA

The principal administrative reason for setting up the WPA
as a federal program was the need for control. The difficulties that Hopkins had faced with the FERA in securing
a satisfactory work program without direct federal control
were still fresh in mind. Likewise, the successful experience
with the CWA as a direct federal program could not be
ignored. The lesson was clear: a federal program would be

preferable if it would win approval.

In the early days of the Depression, Hopkins had been able to manage under the grant-in-aid system of the FERA by taking advantage of the inexperience of the localities and the emergency conditions. His "rules and regulations" were seldom questioned, and his informal use of field represent-atives and a Division of Investigation met little opposition. The states were desperate, had had no experience with large-scale relief, and were willing to accept almost any-thing reasonable that Washington suggested. By 1935, things were different. States had had two years' experience, had a trained staff, and were acting more independently. Ulti-mately, the only formal and effective means of control under the grant-in-aid mechanism (i.e., federalization, or cutting off funds) were politically unattractive. A direct federal program was the answer.

All the WPA officials from Washington down through the operational personnel in the localities were federal officials, and all the WPA workers were paid directly from the United States Treasury. Such a system did not prevent the WPA, however, from becoming a cooperative federal-state-local venture, for the WPA projects generally were proposed, planned, initiated and sponsored by state and local public agencies. [10] One of the problems encoun-tered was that many state legislatures were dominated by rural groups little interested in operating "costly" work programs for the urban unemployed. While part of this problem was obviated by deciding against the grant-in-aid system, Hopkins used direct federal-local contacts increas-ingly in order to deal with city executives who were eager to conduct useful work programs. [11] Federal funds then were earmarked for specific local projects with little if any state involvement. [12]

The projects themselves were staggering in their variety and number. The WPA undertook more than a quarter of

a million, ranging over nearly all fields of economic and
social activity. The overwhelming majority involved construction activities, but this fact would tell only part of the
story of their diversity. For example, within a month after
approval of a $3 million project for site reclamation of an
airport in California, approval was also given for a school
repair project in the same state to cost only $132. [13]
Moreover, in addition to the thousands of similar construction projects, large and small, the WPA was responsible
for taking over the entire function of municipal government
for the bankrupt and desolate city of Key West, Florida.
[14]

Unlike the PWA, which operated almost exclusively on
a contract basis, the WPA carried on almost wholly by the
"force-account" method. This meant that the WPA itself
was responsible for hiring and paying workers, purchasing
the necessary materials, supplies and equipment, and supervising the work done. There were good reasons for this
decision. The WPA, by the very nature of its assignment,
used a high percentage of the unskilled and semiskilled,
many of whom had had no previous experience doing the
jobs now assigned to them. They had been on relief, however, and needed the work more than a contractor's own
labor force. While skilled workmen using laborsaving equipment could have done the work faster and perhaps more
proficiently, Hopkins emphasized that the goals of WPA
were not material—they were social. He wanted to pump
money back into the local communities and a sense of use-
fulness and self-worth into the people. This was a task of
human reconstruction as opposed to physical construction,
and Hopkins always kept that fact foremost in decisions.

For this reason, he abandoned the FERA wage policy
and the "budgetary deficiency" principle. The budgetary
deficiency method required that the worker be treated like
a client: subject to frequent investigation to determine

whether he had outside income which should be deducted, and to counseling on budgeting and proper spending. Hopkins substituted the "security wage," based roughly on wages prevailing in the community for comparable work. The objective was to pay a good cash wage, not high enough to compete with private employment, but a living wage. To compensate for being lower than wages in the private sector, the security wage had the "security" feature: a worker was paid full salary even if, for example, the weather was too severe to work. In the end, it averaged about $50 a month per man, or exactly twice the then current average relief payment per case. [15] Most important, however, was the psychological effect: WPA pay was regarded as wages earned for work done. As one WPA worker proudly reported, "I'm no longer a 'case'; I'm an employee." [16]

The Boondoggle

While the leaf-raking days were over, critics of the new works program wasted no time in harping on the "white-collar" projects. To many observers—congressmen especially—they were the boondoggle of the WPA, a fancier equivalent of the leaf-raking and grass-clipping of the FERA. Hopkins insisted that, in spite of expressed contempt for them, the white-collar projects should continue. In testimony before the House Appropriations Sub-Committee he made a brilliant defense of the principle behind white-collar projects. The dignity of the individual, he argued, was best maintained by devising ways for him to use his skills, trade or profession—and that this precept was just as valid for the artist as for the plumber. [17] In effect, Hopkins' effort was to counter the lingering "work test" mentality of the old poor laws which viewed hard manual labor as the only appropriate role for the able-bodied poor. However, white-collar workers just did not seem to suffer enough to keep some legislators happy.

In addition, among some veteran lawmakers, there was an aversion to the arts and letters (which constituted a large proportion of white-collar projects). [18]   A new road, a bridge repaired, an airport reclaimed—this they could understand; but why, they would argue, do you need to make dictionaries, paint murals, conduct studies and the like? Hopkins made his decision and stood firm. As Hallie Flanagan, head of the Federal Theater Project under the WPA, recalls,

> Hopkins decided that unemployed theater professionals and their fellow musicians, painters and writers could get as hungry as unemployed engineers. He further decided—and this was much more revolutionary—that their skills were as worthy of conservation. [19]

The projects continued and, at the end of the WPA, Hopkins could point with great pride to some of the achievements. Of one he was particularly proud: the invention of the hot lunch for school children. Women working for the WPA peeled the vegetables, cooked the dishes and poured the milk. Later, he remarked, "Educators hope that the school lunch will remain as a device in social education." [20]

The Issues

Several of the decisions implicit in the new works program legislation were subject to widespread criticism. [21]   While some of this criticism was partisan and political, there were issues that transcended party labels.

The first of these was the decision that eligibility for
employment on WPA projects would be based on relief
status. Specifically, at least 90% of the workers had to be
hired from among the employables on the relief rolls. This
rule differed from that governing employment in the CWA
(where Hopkins had deliberately drawn half of the workers
from the FERA rolls and half from those not on relief.)
The explanation for the new decision was simple: the primary objective of the WPA, as stated by the President, was
to put 3½ million employables now on relief rolls back to
work. The President's decision, in turn, had been shaped by
the unwillingness of Congress to grant sufficient funds to
take care of *all* the employables who were looking for
work. As Charles notes,

> Additional funds were what WPA really needed to
> employ more people. Both Congress and the New
> Deal leaders were cautious in appropriations, de-
> siring to keep expenditures within reason, and usu-
> ally hoping the economy of the nation would im-
> prove sufficiently to eliminate federal work relief.
> [22]

As a result, the WPA could not employ all of the unemployed employables from the FERA rolls who had been
certified for WPA jobs. Because of insufficient funds, there
were always 350,000 to 900,000 persons in this category
that should have been hired under the terms of the legislation.

The decision to hire only from the relief rolls, of course,
meant return of the means test and certification—measures
which Hopkins personally opposed and had abolished
effectively in the CWA program. Someone had to attest
to the fact that the potential WPA worker had been on
relief and that his resources were insufficient without federal

aid. Had funds been available, both Roosevelt and Hopkins
would have opted for throwing the program open unquali-
fiedly to all the unemployed.

The decision not to serve the unemployed who had not
been on the FERA rolls met with professional opposition.
"Social workers," said Dorothy Kahn, "advocated a federal
public works program and a federal relief program but they
did not advocate what is now known as WPA—a works program to which the unemployed not on relief are ineligible."
[23]   Gathered at a conference in late 1935, social work
leaders criticized the Administration bitterly for "abandon-
ing all of the unemployed who could not be absorbed into
the work program." [24]   The fact that federal aid for relief of *all* unemployed workers had been included under
the FERA and now was withdrawn without a proper sub-
stitute made them frustrated and angry. In January 1936,
there were only about 3,500,000 people in WPA programs
as against more than 11,000,000 unemployed in the
country.

Clearly, there were tremendous gaps in the new program
that Roosevelt had effected, with many desperate Americans falling between the cracks. The federal government
now, in effect, was taking responsibility in its work programs for only 3½ million of the unemployed, and making
provision in its grants-in-aid for selected categories of the
unemployable through the Social Security Act. Speaking
for the American Association of Social Workers, William
Hodson said:

> The present Social Security Act establishes a [per-
> manent] system for the old and for the young; but
> since the abolition of FERA, no federal assistance is
> provided for that very large group which falls be-
> tween youth and old age, and which, by reason of
> unemployment, and many other causes, is in need

of help and unable to secure a WPA job. [25]

Hodson argued for a permanent system of grants-in-aid to assist the states and localities in carrying out relief for all those not covered by work or social security programs. [26] Without such a federal grant-in-aid program for general public assistance, the state and local governments would be asked to assume an unreasonable burden which, he felt, would bring a certain return to pre-Depression poor law conditions. Edith Abbott, one of the leaders of the social work profession, put the question:

> Back to the states, Mr. Hopkins? Back to the local authorities that have no facilities and no funds for taking care of these people? For going back to the states really means going back to the counties and back to the townships; and back to the inefficiency, incompetency, and inadequacy of the system of poor relief supported by local property taxes. [27]

The social workers were right: the WPA and social security were only part of the package of programs and financial aid that were needed. Over the years the categorical programs were expanded, social insurance was broadened, and private enterprise began to take up the slack in employment. In the meantime, what Roosevelt and Hopkins had put forth indeed had not been a perfect program, but it *had* been one that moved the country forward, setting indelible precedents for the future.

Exit Hopkins

In December 1938, Hopkins left the WPA and the world of relief to become Secretary of Commerce. At that time, the WPA was at its zenith, providing jobs for 3,330,000 persons; but, as war production activities gradually accelerated in late 1939 and in 1940, industry began to absorb the unemployed. [28] The formal order for the liquidation of the WPA was contained in a letter from the President to the new Federal Works Administrator in December 1942. Roosevelt stated that the WPA rolls had decreased to a point where a national work relief program no longer was needed and that project operations should be closed out in as many states as possible by February 1, 1943, and in all states as soon thereafter as possible. [29] As a result, the WPA program ceased operations on June 30, 1943. A Division of Liquidation set up within the Federal Works Agency functioned for one more year to oversee the completion of administrative and contractual obligations.

The WPA had been a social experiment of mammoth proportions. Spending over 10 billion dollars (86 percent on wages), it had given employment to nearly 8,000,000 individuals, one out of five of all the nation's workers. [30] Surveying these achievements, Donald Howard wrote:

> Primary credit for success achieved through the WPA program must, of course, go to President Roosevelt and Harry Hopkins. Without the social vision, deep human sympathies, creative political leadership, and tireless energy of these two peerless friends of the disadvantaged, America's "new approach" to the problem of unemployment might never have been attempted, to say nothing of being successfully executed upon a gigantic and previously undreamed-of scale. [31]

It was not that Hopkins and the WPA were uncontroversial! In June 1939, a Gallup poll asking the public to name the "greatest accomplishment" and also the "worst thing" done by the New Deal found that "relief and the WPA" led *both* counts by a considerable margin. [32]

Any evaluation of the WPA program must take into account the impact of the program on the nation, and polls taken then show that the works program won wide popular support. "At no time during the first five years of WPA's existence," notes one historian, "did a majority of the people indicate a desire to abandon WPA. Usually from 54 to 90% thought WPA should continue." [33] Moreover, despite some heated confrontations, Hopkins and his agency maintained the support of the majority of the Congress right up until World War II. The program never became the "major campaign issue" that Hopkins' chief rival, Harold Ickes, had predicted. The American people gave Roosevelt and the New Deal Democrats resounding victories at the polls in the elections in 1936, 1938 and 1940.

What was the WPA? Cabell Phillips says it was "more than just a New Deal device to make jobs for the jobless. It was a major phenomenon—the symbol and principal engine of the New Deal social revolution." [34] This is probably true. And if so, it would seem to make Harry Hopkins—social revolutionary—an extraordinary architect and a brilliant engineer.

NOTES

1. Harry L. Hopkins, "The Future of Relief," *New Republic,* February 10, 1937, p. 9.
2. Hopkins, *Spending to Save,* p. 109.
3. Sherwood, *Roosevelt and Hopkins,* p. 65.
4. Such large-scale public works were not without precedent. More than 2,400 years before the Christian Era, the rulers of Egypt were faced with the question of employing idle labor. It was answered

with the most widespread and effective public construction program the world up to that time had known. The Nile was harnessed. Irrigation lakes and canals, public buildings and monuments, entire cities were built on a nationwide scale—forty-three centuries ago.

5. It was a customary wedding of ideas: something old (return of the unemployables to the care of states and/or localities) and something new (the federal government sharing in the cost); something borrowed (the grant-in-aid mechanism) and something blue (a pool of funds—OASI—to be administered federally as an insurance trust).

6. Roosevelt appointed Frank Walker as Administrator of the Division on Applications and Information; Harold Ickes to head the Advisory Committee on Allotments; and Harry Hopkins to oversee the Works Progress operation.

7. Executive Order No. 7034, May 6, 1935.

8. In subsequent Congressional testimony, Hopkins said the actual cost of giving a man a job for one month on WPA had averaged $82, of which $18.50 was paid by the project sponsor and $63.50 by the federal government. Later, Ickes submitted a report showing that the cost of providing one month's work to a man on a PWA project averaged $350—or more than four times the cost under Hopkins' WPA. See U. S. Congress, House Committee on Appropriations, 75th Cong., 3d Sess., *Hearings...on Emergency Relief Appropriation Act of 1938*, p. 17 (re: Hopkins); p. 395 (re: Ickes).

9. Macmahon, Millett and Ogden, *Federal Work Relief*, p. 123.

10. The sole exceptions were a few federal projects—mostly white-collar—sponsored by the WPA itself, comprising only about 3 percent of the estimated cost of all the WPA projects.

11. Burns and Williams, *Work, Security and Relief*, p. 56; and see Edward A. and J. Kerwin Williams, "The WPA Method vs. Grants-in-Aid," *Survey Midmonthly*, LXXVI (March 1940), pp. 91-93.

12. The Allotment Board of the WPA did provide a little known alternative to federal funding and supervision. Any state, city or county government which wanted to run its own WPA program *and* would appropriate a certain sum of money for carrying out the program was entitled to receive matching funds from federal appropriations and to run its projects without further federal intervention. The State of Wisconsin and the City of Baltimore took preliminary steps to adopt this procedure but never completed the requirements. The WPA, therefore, retained its purely federal status throughout, with the federal government in control of the selection and administration

of all state and local projects. See Paul V. Betters, J. Kerwin Williams, and Sherwood L. Reeder, *Recent Federal-City Relations* (Washington: U. S. Conference of Mayors, 1936), pp. 90-91.

13. For a detailed account of the wide range of WPA projects see Donald S. Howard, *The WPA and Federal Relief Policy* (New York: Russell Sage Foundation, 1943), pp. 125-28.

14. Cabell Phillips, *From the Crash to the Blitz: 1929-1939* (New York: The Macmillan Co., 1969), p. 278.

15. Macmahon, Millett and Ogden, *Federal Work Relief*, p. 149. The "security wage" principle was in effect during the initial year of the WPA program. These security wages actually varied from $19 a month for unskilled labor in the rural South to $94 a month for technical and professional people in urban areas of the North and West. See Burns and Williams, *Work, Security and Relief*, p. 61.

16. Letter, Lorena Hickok to Harry Hopkins, n.d., Hopkins MSS, Hyde Park Collection.

17. Testimony of Harry L. Hopkins, *Hearings*, Sub-Committee of House Committee on Appropriations, 74th Cong., 2d Sess., on H. R. 12624, April 8, 1936, pp. 102-09.

18. See Jerre G. Mangione, *The Dream and the Deal: The Federal Writers' Project, 1935-1943* (Boston: Little, Brown Co., 1972).

19. Hallie Flanagan, "The Drama of the Federal Theater Project," in Howard Zinn, ed., *New Deal Thought* (Indianapolis, Ind.: Bobbs-Merrill Co., 1966), p. 173.

20. Hopkins, *Spending to Save*, p. 171.

21. The five most common arguments advanced against the works program were that it: was too costly compared to direct relief; encouraged people to refuse private employment; sponsored useless projects; was essentially political; and served only to build a huge bureaucracy in Washington. These criticisms were refuted in Harry L. Hopkins, "The WPA Looks Forward," *Survey Midmonthly*, LXXIV (June 1938), pp. 195-98.

22. Charles, *Minister of Relief*, p. 232.

23. Dorothy C. Kahn, "The Occasion for This Conference" in *This Business of Relief, Proceedings of the Delegate Conference, American Association of Social Workers, February 14, 1936* (New York: American Association of Social Workers, 1936), p. 23.

24. See Grace Abbott, "Social Workers and Public Welfare Departments," and Harry Greenstein, "Work Programs and Relief Measures" in *This Business of Relief*, pp. 15-24 and pp. 69-77.

25. William Hodson, "Clearing the Lines of Responsibility" in

This Business of Relief, p. 109.

26. For a detailed outline of the AASW recommendations see "Outline for a Federal Assistance Program," Appendix I, *This Business of Relief,* pp. 162-69.

27. Edith Abbott, "Don't Do It, Mr. Hopkins!" *Nation,* January 9, 1935, p. 41.

28. On July 1, 1939 the Works Progress Administration was renamed the Work Projects Administration and made part of the new Federal Works Agency. (Public Resolution No. 20, 76th Cong., June 7, 1939).

29. Letter, President Roosevelt to Philip Fleming, December 4, 1942, General Subject Series, WPA Central Files, National Archives.

30. Federal Works Agency, *Summary of Relief and Federal Work Program Statistics* (Washington: U. S. Government Printing Office, 1941) is a complete statistical summary of the WPA. For a detailed account of the work of the WPA see Howard, *Federal Relief Policy;* Brown, *Public Relief;* and Burns and Williams, *Work, Security and Relief.*

31. Howard, *Federal Relief Policy,* p. 841.

32. Wecter, *Age of the Great Depression,* p. 294.

33. Charles, *Minister of Relief,* p. 235. In addition, scholarly studies have given the WPA a relatively good bill of health, generally concluding it was "effective" and "well administered." See Howard, *Federal Relief Policy,* p. 847.

34. Phillips, *Crash to Blitz,* p. 276.

Part III

MANY ROLES, MANY DUTIES

From the cradle to the grave they ought to be in a social insurance system.

Franklin D. Roosevelt

We are in a new fight...the war to insure economic and social security to every citizen of this country.

Harry L. Hopkins

7. To Campaign for a Cause

Introduction

HOPKINS characteristically would fight for what he believed and his battles of the 1930s took many forms. Five of those battles are historically important, representative, and relevant to the politics of social welfare administration. They include Hopkins' role in the development of social insurance; his feud with Ickes; his participation in partisan politics; his advocacy for work programs; and his role in the defense of the forgotten Americans.

Work Relief vs. The Dole

By and large, the business community preferred direct relief over work relief, and either one of the two over a program of public works. The reasons were twofold: first, they feared that government competition for labor would force an increase in wages; second, they usually tended to opt for whatever program was cheaper. Since direct relief (the dole) was by far the least expensive program, it was preferred by most corporate leaders; if the choice were work relief (as under the second phase of the FERA) or public works (as under the WPA), the former

would be desired because it cut costs to a minimum and
would prove least competitive with wages and labor supply
in the private sector. It was simply a matter of economics.
Industrial leaders, accustomed to being courted by government in the Harding, Coolidge and Hoover administrations,
expected similar treatment from Roosevelt and Hopkins.
The business of the nation, after all, was business.

The New Deal leaders looked at the question another
way. They were less interested in what was cheapest than
they were in what was best for the people, and what the
people wanted. As Roosevelt told Congress in January
1935,

> The lessons of history confirmed by the evidence
> immediately before me, show conclusively that
> continued dependence upon relief induces a spirit-
> ual and moral disintegration fundamentally de-
> structive to the national fibre. To dole out relief in
> this way is to administer a narcotic, a subtle de-
> stroyer of the human spirit. It is inimical to the
> dictates of sound policy. It is in violation of the
> traditions of America. Work must be found for
> the able-bodied but destitute workers. [1]

To this Hopkins added his belief that people in America
have a conviction that there is something intrinsically good
in earning a living:

> It is, in fact, such a deep-seated conviction that
> without work men actually go to pieces. They lose
> the respect of their wives, sons and daughters be-
> cause they lose respect for themselves, even though
> they have broken no laws and even though their
> deportment as fathers and neighbors continues to
> be above reproach. [2]

Why spend four billion dollars on employment, he was asked? Would it not be cheaper to keep on with the doles?

> Of course it would be cheaper in terms of money! Cheaper, in all probability, by a full 50 percent; but, when you count up in terms of pride, courage, self-respect, ambition and energy, a direct-relief program is a thousand times more costly than a work program, for it tends inevitably towards the creation of a permanent pauper class, hopeless and helpless, an increasing and crushing weight on the backs of the gainfully employed.... [3]

Both Roosevelt and Hopkins were arguing eloquently that a works program was best for the American people.

Hopkins was equally concerned with what the people wanted. In a democracy, he believed, it was dangerous to make decisions based only on what is best for the people. They must tell their leaders what they prefer, and those in high places must listen. At a Senate hearing on the new works program legislation, Hopkins was asked specifically if a large percentage of the people then on direct relief wanted work instead, to which he replied:

> All of them. The number of people that do not want to work on the relief rolls is so infinitesimal... in number that it is not important. One of the interesting things we have learned from this depression is that the old poor law theory that the way to keep a person from getting relief is to offer him a job, is absolutely fallacious...all of these people want work. [4]

Hopkins continued to fight for work programs, and his battles were marked with victories at almost every turn.

He not only knew what was best for people, but knew what the people wanted. In the end, it was his conviction that the able-bodied person's wish for work was so basic that it should be translated into a social right. "Recovery connotes to me a policy of reconstruction," he wrote, "in which the social order will be amended to include the right of people to work..." [5] Hopkins fought tirelessly for this concept.

Economic Security—for Whom?

In most of western Europe, social insurance in one form or another had existed for a generation before 1930, while in the United States it was still a novel idea, repugnant to many as demeaning the doctrine of self-reliance and to still others as erecting the dreaded signpost of creeping socialism. The experiences with the early Depression programs of relief, however, led Roosevelt to take the first step toward a long-range program of social security. On June 29, 1934, he appointed a five-member Committee on Economic Security to make recommendations and proposals which would promote greater economic and social security for the nation. [6] The Committee and staff worked diligently, and in six months submitted their recommendations to the President. These suggestions became the basis for the country's first federal social insurance legislation, enacted in August 1935. [7] The Social Security Act included a system of unemployment insurance under joint state-federal control; a system of old-age pensions under federal control; and a permanent program of federal grants-in-aid to the states for aid to the aged, dependent children and the blind.

During the summer of 1934, Hopkins took an extended trip to Europe. Roosevelt had encouraged him to do so for his health, and also because, as a member of the Committee on Economic Security, Hopkins could gather some information from foreign officials on their social insurance programs. John Kingsbury, Hopkins' supervisor and mentor in his earliest years as a social worker in New York, had just returned from England where he had held a long interview with Beatrice and Sidney Webb, the Fabian leaders who had been members of the 1905 Royal Commission on the Poor Law in England. Kingsbury wrote that in view of "the strategic importance of your position" (in planning for the future of social insurance in America), Hopkins should himself talk with the Webbs on his European tour. In addition, Kingsbury enclosed a confidential memorandum on his own interview with the Webbs which urged strong moves toward some of the more "radical" provisions (of the nature Hopkins would later recommend to the committee). [8]

When Hopkins returned from Europe, he went right to work in drafting his ideas. Arthur Altmeyer tells us that, next to the Chairwoman, Frances Perkins, Hopkins played the most active role on the committee among all the members. [9] In the months ahead he actually drafted many of the ideas which were later incorporated into the social security legislation. As Chandler suggests, it now was clear that Hopkins had become "the most influential man in the Administration in the broad fields of social welfare *and* social insurance." [10]

Hopkins waged three battles within the committee that are of historical importance. First, he urged that the aid to dependent children program be broadened to include children of unemployed parents, as well as children dependent because of the death, disability or absence from the home of a parent. He stressed the need for this added provision because the unemployment insurance plan would include only those actually employed and able to contribute. Fresh from the experience of the Depression, Hopkins was aware of the large sector of the population that could be excluded from a social insurance plan because no member of the family had a sufficient record as a participant in the world of work. In the end, however, the committee rejected his suggestion, and the country was to wait three more decades until Hopkins' farsighted proposal was translated into law.

Second, the staff of the committee recommended that the old-age and insurance taxes and benefits be limited to industrial and commercial workers, excluding persons engaged in agriculture and domestic service. Hopkins was bitterly opposed and Edwin Witte, the staff director, tells us that Hopkins was successful in personally convincing the committee members to make the old-age benefits applicable to all employed persons. "This change," Witte states, "was made largely at the insistence of Mr. Hopkins...." [11] In the end, the change met strong opposition in the Congress and was deleted from the final legislation. Again, Hopkins had been ahead of his time, and the inclusion of agricultural and domestic workers did not come until several years after his death, in the 1950 and 1954 Social Security Act amendments.

Finally, Hopkins led the fight for legislating a program of compulsory health insurance. The health field had been an area of particular interest ever since his work as director of the New York Tuberculosis and Health Association. In March 1934, two months before Roosevelt had appointed the Committee on Economic Security, Hopkins had said:

> I am convinced that with one bold stroke we could carry the American people with us, not only for unemployment insurance but for sickness and health insurance, and that it could be done in the next

eighteen months if we only have the courage to go
after it and do it. [12]

Later that fall, he took his idea to the Committee on
Economic Security and declared that they ought to come
out "not only for unemployment insurance but for sickness and health insurance as well." [13] "Mr. Hopkins
was always of the opinion that health insurance was by far
the most valuable form of social insurance," recalls Witte;
and he rapidly became "more interested in health insurance" than any other single phase of the proposed program. [14]   However, Hopkins lost once again. The
recommendation was never sustained, largely because of
the intense pressure of the American Medical Association.
In consultation with the President, committee staff decided that A.M.A. opposition to compulsory health insurance was so strong that its inclusion might endanger passage
of the Social Security Act as a whole.

Amid all of the victories that Hopkins enjoyed during
his career in federal relief, he thus had defeats as well. He
seemed to have an extraordinary capacity to do battle,
retaining his original strength and convictions, win or lose.
With these three skirmishes relative to social security, he
would appear, in retrospect, to have been prophetic in his
wisdom. But it is not only important that he was right; it
is also crucial that Harry Hopkins had the dedication,
courage and tenacity to take an idea he believed in and
carry it as far as it would go.

The Forgotten Americans

The 1920s had been harsh years for many Americans who
were not fortunate enough to be part of the luxury and
gaiety of the era. When the Depression came at the close

of the decade, certain groups of neglected Americans were in a particularly disadvantaged position to fend for themselves, even with the new relief programs. For many of these groups, Hopkins became a champion of their cause, helping in a small way to change the course of history by his actions.

Hopkins felt particularly moved by the plight of "transients" who were excluded from many state and local programs. In response, he established a special transient program within the FERA, and placed it under the supervision of his most trusted lieutenant, Aubrey Williams. This program pioneered in obliterating the concept of "legal settlement" which had effectively barred service to so many of the destitute in the nation.

Founded in English Poor Law and the manorial system, the legal settlement laws were state statutes that required residency as a condition for receipt of public assistance and support. They typically mandated a certain period of residence (usually within the state for at least one year, within the county for six months)—and stipulated further that absence from the state for a specified time would invalidate legal settlement. Before the FERA, these laws disenfranchised a whole segment of the population; during the Depression, when people were moving from state to state in a desperate search for work, the problem of transiency and the principle of legal settlement came into sharp conflict. Laid off their jobs as factories began to close, more and more men were moving their families great distances in search of employment. When they were unsuccessful, due to the nationwide severity of the Depression, they frequently found that state residency requirements barred them from relief in their present location. By then they were trapped because absence from their "home" state probably meant loss of "legal settlement" there, as well; in addition, most families were far too destitute to

consider the long trip home. Consequently, thousands of
Americans were on the roads and on the rails.

The Transient Division of the FERA began to function
in July of 1933, just two months after the relief program
had started. Hopkins gave this effort considerable personal
attention. He circumvented the residency requirements inherent in the laws of legal settlement by "nationalizing"
the fiscal responsibility for transiency through federal provision. [15] Toward the end of 1933, forty states and the
District of Columbia had qualified for federal funds to aid
transients; by December of that year, they were caring for
approximately 228,000 transient persons. [16] Thirty-five
years later the Supreme Court would declare residency
requirements unconstitutional, but Harry Hopkins was not
one to wait for court decisions. [17]

Hopkins recognized early the particular plight of black
citizens. In a special directive to all state and local FERA
administrations, Hopkins formally stated that there was to
be no discrimination "because of race, religion, color, non-
citizenship, political affiliation, or because of membership
in any special or selected group." [18] Of all the categories
above, those of race and color became the most generally
debated—not only in the Deep South, but in the Middle
West and Central States as well. Hopkins continued his
fight for equal rights for black citizens in the WPA with
two more administrative orders barring discrimination
against workers "who are qualified by training and experience to be assigned to work projects." [19] "Largely as
a result of these determined efforts," writes Raymond
Wolters in his definitive study of race relations during the
Depression, "the share of WPA jobs going to Negro workers
during the late 1930s and early 1940s exceeded their proportion in the general population." [20] As a result, the
WPA in January 1936 had 30 percent black workers, and,
unlike the Civilian Conservation Corps, had no quotas. [21]

Hopkins and his staff persisted in their efforts to end racial discrimination in relief. In many cases they fought bitter battles with local officials, but insisted on the right of black people to equal benefits and wages. There is much correspondence to suggest that the civil rights battle was among the roughest of all the battles in which Hopkins engaged, and that his refusal to give in under political pressures was a tremendous gain for black people and black institutions. [22]

The NAACP's *Crisis* said of Hopkins and the WPA:

> ...they have made great gains for the race in areas which heretofore have set their faces steadfastly against decent relief for Negroes. [23]

The civil rights revolution would not come until the 1960s, but even in the 1930s, Hopkins was conducting a quiet, modest little revolution of his own. [24]

Hopkins did not strike out at the South, in particular, for he held a remarkable understanding for the special needs of this neglected region of America. He had spent more than four years with the Red Cross in Atlanta and New Orleans where he had gained an empathic understanding of the economic plight and corresponding social needs of the area. In addition, three of five FERA divisions were headed by southerners who kept Hopkins constantly in touch with southern problems: Aubrey Williams, a native of Montgomery, Alabama; Lawrence Westbrook, formerly relief administrator in Texas; and Mrs. Ellen Woodward, long active in social welfare and politics in Mississippi. Each of these trusted aides represented the new progressive element in the South and served not only as key advisers to Hopkins on regional questions but also as links with a section of the country which, by tradition, had an element of distrust and suspicion toward federal programs.

This was a "southern strategy" all his own and proved to be an influential factor in the smooth-working relationships that developed between southern officials and Washington.

An early decision Hopkins made to establish scholarships to train some of the FERA staff at schools of social work also benefited the South because he excluded the Northeastern states that had a relatively large number of trained staffs. Miss Elizabeth Wisner, then Dean of the Tulane University School of Social Work in New Orleans, recalls talking with Hopkins about his plan:

> I was, of course, delighted by such a proposal as the Southern schools of social work were struggling with a very small enrollment and little or no scholarships. In the end nearly a million dollars was spent on this program. It had a direct impact on the South where many young women and some young men from the smaller towns and rural areas had their first contact with social welfare programs. [25]

Miss Wisner concluded that this program was "the greatest single contribution to the development of social work that has been made in this area of the country," and provided an important nucleus of workers in the South with some professional preparation for the public assistance and child welfare programs when the Social Security Act was passed in 1935. [26]

Thus Hopkins kept in touch with the South, its special needs and regional problems, making a conspicuous effort to adapt his program to help a long neglected portion of the country. Southerners, like transients and minorities, often were neglected Americans—and Hopkins worked energetically in their behalf.

Hopkins and Ickes

The feud between Harold Ickes and Harry Hopkins is
something of a legend. There can be no question that the
conflict was genuine, that it persisted for many years, and
that there never was a resolution satisfactory to both
parties. For those interested in the historical evolution of
the vendetta, much has been written. [27]

Hopkins and Ickes held certain principles in common.
Both were progressives with an unimpeachable reputation
as liberals. Most important, they were devoted to President
Roosevelt and both were firmly committed to the policies
of the New Deal.

In personality and temperament, however, they were
a study in contrast. Hopkins saw Ickes as slow-moving,
cautious and generally unresponsive, a compulsive little
man who was thoroughly disagreeable to work with, and
"out of the question" as a friend. Ickes, on the other hand,
found Hopkins to be an irresponsible, "lawless individual,"
wanting to arrogate power to himself at the expense of
others. He viewed Hopkins as intolerant and impetuous;
said Ickes, "I never knew anyone more sure of his own
judgment." [28]

Perhaps conflict was inevitable when Roosevelt established *two* relief-centered agencies in 1933, even though
every effort was made to separate the nature of their
duties. After all, Ickes, as head of the PWA, ran a work
program, and Hopkins, with the FERA, ran a program of
small projects and relief. But by November of that year,
Roosevelt felt more had to be done to get people back to
work and that Ickes' PWA was progressing too slowly to
carry the country through the winter. His decision was to
divert $400,000,000 (from the $3,300,000,000 which
Congress had granted to the PWA earlier that year) to set
up the new CWA under Hopkins. The President made the

decision based on his estimate of the overall needs of the nation; but to Ickes, this was "robbing Harold to pay Harry," and soon the conflict came out in the open.

When the CWA ended in the spring of 1934, the tension subsided. But soon Roosevelt once again realized that the PWA could not get underway the necessary and extensive program because of the unavoidable yet time-consuming process of planning, designing and reviewing projects, clearing up legal matters, advertising for bids and letting contracts. Roosevelt needed a new and more responsive system that would put men to work and give a stimulus to consumer purchasing power. Yet the President valued Ickes' honesty and his ability to produce durable public works. The solution was typically FDR: he would establish a new works program, leaving Ickes and Hopkins both actively involved and competing with one another. He would create "a planetary system wherein many would have a place in the sun." [29]

As with most compromises, no one was entirely happy. Treasury Secretary Morgenthau felt that Hopkins alone should have the voice in making all public work and relief decisions. [30]   Ickes was deeply disappointed. Hopkins saw the potential for the WPA implicit in the right to carry on "small useful projects" and was not troubled. Others, like the FERA's Corrington Gill, saw the WPA and the PWA as working hand-in-hand, as complementary, non-competing programs:

> They serve different functions: one is primarily a materials purchasing program designed to stimulate heavy industry, the other is primarily an employment program and a means of sustaining purchasing power. [31]

While Gill was right in theory, in practice the programs

proved competitive as well, setting the stage for a basic confrontation between Ickes and Hopkins that would reveal much about both men.

That Hopkins "won" the battle with Ickes—and most observers would agree he did—is not so important as understanding the nature of the victory. It would be easy to personalize the conflict and view it simply as a feud between good men of different temperaments; or, to see it as a conflict between competing programs in the same general market—the conflict of Lever Brothers and Procter and Gamble, Gimbels and Macy's. The answer does not seem so simple, for the truth would appear to be that Hopkins and Ickes were selling different products.

The crucial difference between the two men was not one of personality but of ideology. Ickes' point of view was that of a businessman. He believed that the best way to relieve unemployment on a long-range basis was to "prime the pump" by subsidizing private enterprise for the construction of massive, self-liquidating projects. Hopkins' approach was that of a social worker. He believed that the main object was to get the greatest number of people to work in the shortest space of time, and that the productivity of the work they performed was of secondary importance. "I happen to believe," said Ickes, "that secondary employment is more important than [immediate] employment at the site." [32]   But try to find an unemployed man who would agree! When an adviser came to Hopkins with a project that would take a long time to get into operation, but which, he promised, would work out "in the long run" an angry Hopkins replied:"People don't *eat* in the long run; they eat every day."

Ickes tended to be more interested in the product than the person making it. Referring to the white-collar projects, Luther Gulick suggests figuratively that Ickes would want to inspect every piece of art to see if it were good; Hopkins would take a look at the pride on the artist's face and say, "I don't care; just put a frame on it." [33] Hopkins would not be interested in what the picture was worth, but what returning to his source of livelihood meant for the artist and his family. In contrast, James Burns writes of Ickes:

> Suspicious, cantankerous and stubborn, he authorized projects only after he had satisfied himself as to their legal propriety, economic value and engineering practicality. [34]

Raymond Moley illustrates the point well:

> Ickes and Hopkins are significant as counterpoint between one man who understood the psychological needs of the nation and one who did not. Even if Ickes was overcautious to the point of paranoia, this personality trait was less damaging than his inability to comprehend human behavior and common human needs. [35]

The second area of conflict in ideology was political. If Hopkins were not a better administrator, he certainly was a better politician in the sense of correctly judging the will of the people. Ickes' measure for weighing the political prudence of a plan was to determine "how tight a ship could be maintained," whether there could possibly be any inefficiencies, and what would be the reaction of the members of Congress. The day after they both had presented their proposed work programs to Roosevelt, Ickes wrote in his diary:

> I have no confidence myself in Hopkins' program. I think it is the greatest present threat to the President's re-election. It looks to me as if the WPA will

> be perhaps the major issue in the campaign next
> year. Its absurdities, its inefficiencies, its insuffi-
> ciencies, its bunglings and its graftings will be aired
> in the press and from the platform and I don't see
> how we can defend it. [36]

Ickes' political ideas were shadowed by an inability to
understand the wishes of the *people* (not the Congress or
the press), and the willingness and capacity that one must
have to translate these wishes into programs. Men back at
work—for whatever cost and by whatever program—were
certain to have a positive feeling about Roosevelt. This was,
in fact, the lesson in political democracy that ruled in
November, just as Roosevelt and Hopkins had expected.

In short, the feud between Ickes and Hopkins was ideo-
logical, not personal. The sickness of the country was not
just in the economy but in the minds and hopes and hearts
of men, and this was what Hopkins was out to cure. People
had to be given some reason to believe in democracy and in
themselves, not next year, but now. A full-time social
worker and a sometime politician, Hopkins was aware that
the greatest resource of the nation was its people, and the
elected leader who forgot that would not be around long
enough to make the same mistake twice.

Politics or Public Welfare

Hopkins had come to public service from years in the private
social welfare field and shared a conviction (strongly felt in
the voluntary sector) that politics and public welfare should
not mix. Guided by this maxim, Hopkins kept politics to
a minimum in the FERA. Both the Washington and regional
field offices were staffed from the outset with social
workers, economists and public administrators who were
determined to keep political influence over the program

out, and to set a highly professional, nonpartisan framework for relief administration.

In his appointments, Hopkins resisted patronage and nepotism. Moreover, he insisted that staff members never use their public office or public funds for partisan political ends. His policy represented the separation of politics and administration in the best sense, and set an example for the state and local public welfare departments which were being organized under the FERA throughout the country. He brooked no interference in this matter and struck back whenever attempts at political abuse came to his attention. In one instance, where investigation had shown that employees of the North Dakota relief administration were being assessed for political contributions, Hopkins "federalized" relief for North Dakota with the President's personal approval. [37]

Hopkins' administration of the CWA was equally non-political. Appointments were not partisan, notes Schlesinger, and "were as likely to turn up a Democratic culprit as a Republican." [38] Moreover, Stanley High concludes,

> From a considerable amount of personal observation, I should say that this administrative army has fewer lame ducks and superannuates in it than any organization which the government of the United States has sponsored in a good many decades. [39]

In time, however, political pressure began to tell. The turning point came when a very political Congress took its revenge on Hopkins and tacked on an amendment to the 1935 Emergency Relief Appropriations Act legislation requiring Senate confirmation for all WPA positions paying over $5,000 a year. From this moment on, Hopkins was realistic enough to know he was beaten and that his administration of the WPA could not mirror the nonpartisan example he had established in the FERA and CWA programs. Now every appointment would have to be cleared with the Democratic National Committee and local U.S. Senators. Hopkins tried conscientiously to keep the WPA immune to political interference for a while, "but when he found that this could not be done (the effort was hopeless by 1936), he played the game with the subtle craftsmanship of an expert." [40] Hopkins said,

> I thought at first I could be completely non-political. Then they told me I had to be part non-political and part political. I found that was impossible, at least for me. I finally realized that there was nothing for it but to be all-political. [41]

So the social worker became politically active from that point on.

Hopkins made one major trip that fall of 1936 through the West on behalf of the presidential campaign and was very effective. Even James Farley (who cared little for Hopkins' campaigning) admitted that he had proven an extraordinarily effectual interpreter of the New Deal programs. [42] Based on this success, Hopkins publicly supported candidates for office in 1938, and attempted to "purge" conservative Democrats who had voted against the social programs of the Administration.

Thomas E. Dewey makes repeated claims that WPA workers were soliciting for campaign contributions in the 1938 elections all over the country, threatening workers with being dropped from the WPA rolls if they would not cooperate. [43] While the records do not bear this out, the charge of "politics" in the WPA was not without some foundation. Alleged scandals became regular fare for the newspapers and magazines, especially as the November elections approached. Indeed, a noted syndicated columnist,

Thomas L. Stokes, won the Pulitzer Prize for journalism in 1938 for an investigative series on how Senator Alben Barkley of Kentucky "bought" his reelection with WPA funds. [44] There can be little question that the 1939 Hatch Act was a direct outgrowth of this exposé (just as the assassination of President Garfield by a disappointed office-seeker had precipitated the Pendleton Act of 1883.)

Hopkins' involvement in politics led to his own personal political ambitions. In an article for *Forum* in December 1937, the well-known columnist Raymond Clapper discussed the question of Hopkins' ambitions for the presidency. [45] It would seem that Hopkins did entertain presidential aspirations, and Robert Sherwood points out that one of the last requests Hopkins made before his death was that there should be no attempt to disguise the fact that he once had ambitions for the highest office. [46] There is considerable debate among historians and biographers as to whether Roosevelt encouraged Hopkins in this regard in the likelihood that he would not choose to run again in 1940 for a third term. Although most writers appear to take Roosevelt's "encouragement" of Hopkins seriously, there are several dissenters. Moley writes:

> He [Roosevelt] never seriously considered any other candidate....His casual notations of Harry Hopkins' assets and liabilities, solemnly presented by Robert E. Sherwood in his *Roosevelt and Hopkins* as serious evidence that he favored his good friend, can be discounted. This encouragement was merely a way he had in friendly dawdling with intimates....He knew, and Hopkins should have known, that the idea was preposterous. [47]

Speaking as Sherwood's close friend and mentor, Samuel I. Rosenman also feels the biographer here was being naïve, that Roosevelt's intentions never were serious, and that Hopkins himself probably was not quite so serious either. [48]   Arthur Krock further confirms Moley's and Rosenman's positions; Krock recalls that he and the President's Press Secretary, Stephen Early, knew that Roosevelt was only "kidding" Hopkins in this regard. [49]   Rosenman concludes with a feeling that even if Hopkins *himself* had political ambitions—and here we have to take Hopkins at his word—"it is important that it never seriously affected his professional performance." [50]

In the final analysis, the evolution and maturation of Harry Hopkins as a public official shows an increasing political awareness and involvement. He trusted in the representative, democratic process of governing fervently, and

> sincerely believed that unless an administrator in such a position could carry with him the elected politicians, low and high, he failed in the task of conducting public management in the context of democracy. [51]

NOTES

1. Franklin D. Roosevelt, "Message to Joint Session of Congress," January 4, 1935, in Rosenman, *Public Papers,* IV, p. 19.

2. Harry L. Hopkins, "Relief Through Work Demanded by Hopkins," *New York Times,* March 10, 1935, Section E, p. 5.

3. Harry L. Hopkins, "They'd Rather Work," *Collier's,* November 16, 1935, p. 7.

4. U. S. Senate Committee on Appropriations, *Hearings on H. J. Res. 117,* 74th Cong., 1st Sess., 1935, p. 106. Three years later Hopkins spoke before a Special Senate Committee to Investigate Unemployment and Relief. His convictions had not changed and he spoke equally as firmly. "On the matter of a work program as against direct relief, it is my conviction, and one of the strongest convictions

I hold, that the Federal Government should never return to a direct relief program....We should do away with direct relief for the unemployed in the United States."

5. Harry L. Hopkins, "The War on Distress," *Today*, I (December 16, 1933), p. 32.

6. Members were the Secretaries of the Treasury, Agriculture and Labor, the Attorney General, and the Administrator of the FERA. Frances Perkins, the Secretary of Labor, chaired the committee. For a detailed discussion of the work of this committee, see Daniel S. Sanders, *The Impact of Reform Movements on Social Policy Change* (Fair Lawn, N. J.: R. E. Burdick, Inc., 1973), pp. 60 ff.

7. The report of the Committee on Economic Security was transmitted to the Congress by the President in a special message of January 17, 1935. The Economic Security Bill was introduced in the House and Senate simultaneously at that time and became law as the Social Security Act on August 14, 1935. (Pub. Law No. 74-271, 74th Congress). It was not until February 1936, however, that funds for the Social Security Board were appropriated by Congress. See Brown, *Public Relief*, Ch. 13.

8. Letter, John Kingsbury to Harry Hopkins, July 17, 1934, Kingsbury MSS, Library of Congress.

9. Arthur J. Altmeyer, *The Formative Years of Social Security* (Madison: University of Wisconsin Press, 1966), p. 23.

10. Lester V. Chandler, *America's Greatest Depression, 1929-1941* (New York: Harper and Row, 1970), p. 191. (Italics added).

11. Edwin Witte, *Development of the Social Security Act* (Madison: University of Wisconsin Press, 1962), p. 152.

12. Harry L. Hopkins, "Health Planning in the Recovery Program," address to the Advisory Council, Milbank Memorial Fund, March 12, 1934, p. 8. (Unpublished manuscript, Hopkins' Speeches File, FERA Papers, National Archives.)

13. Arthur Schlesinger, Jr., *The Coming of the New Deal* (Boston: Houghton Mifflin Co., 1958), p. 307. See also, Harry L. Hopkins, "Social Planning for the Future," *Social Service Review*, VIII (September 1934), p. 401.

14. Witte, *Development of the Social Security Act*, p. 174; p. 187.

15. See Hopkins, *Spending to Save*, Ch. VI.

16. Betters, Williams and Reeder, *Federal-City Relations*, p. 77.

17. Shapiro *v.* Thompson, 394 U.S. 619, Sup. Ct. April 21, 1969. For discussion see Margaret K. Rosenheim, "Shapiro *v.* Thompson: The Beggars Are Coming to Town," in *Supreme Court Review, 1969,*

ed. Philip B. Kurland (Chicago: University of Chicago Press, 1969).

18. Federal Emergency Relief Administration, *Rules and Regulations No. 3*, July 11, 1933.

19. Work Progress Administration, *Administrative Orders Nos. 41 and 44*, June 22, 1936 and July 11, 1936.

20. Raymond Wolters, *Negroes and the Great Depression* (Westport, Conn.: Greenwood Publishing Co., 1970), p. 204.

21. Carl N. Degler, ed., *The New Deal* (Chicago: Quadrangle Books, 1970), p. 14.

22. See Letter from Lorena Hickok to Harry Hopkins, January 16, 1934, Hopkins MSS, Hyde Park Collection.

23. "The Campaign," *Crisis*, November 1936.

24. For an excellent, balanced collection of articles regarding the effect of the New Deal recovery program on black Americans see Zinn, *New Deal Thought*, Part IX.

25. Letter, Elizabeth Wisner to author, March 14, 1970.

26. Letter, Elizabeth Wisner to Josephine Brown, April 1, 1935, New Subject File, FERA MSS, National Archives.

27. For one of the detailed accounts of the feud, see Charles, *Minister of Relief*, Ch. VI.

28. Harold Ickes, *The Secret Diary of Harold L. Ickes* (New York: Simon and Schuster, 1953), I, pp. 348, 410, 434.

29. Macmahon, Millett and Ogden, *Federal Work Relief*, p. 69.

30. John M. Blum, *From the Morgenthau Diaries: Years of Crises, 1928-1938* (Boston: Houghton Mifflin Co., 1959), p. 245.

31. Corrington Gill, *Wasted Manpower* (New York: W.W. Norton Co., 1939), p. 271.

32. Ickes, *Secret Diary*, I, p. 438.

33. Interview with Luther H. Gulick, December 4, 1969.

34. James M. Burns, *Roosevelt: The Lion and the Fox* (New York: Harcourt, Brace and Co., 1956), p. 196.

35. Interview with Raymond Moley, March 26, 1970.

36. Ickes, *Secret Diary*, I, p. 438.

37. Control in this instance was held by the FERA Washington office from March 1, 1934 to December 15, 1935. For the authority to take over state programs in such situations see FERA Act of 1933, Section 3(b), and Pub. Law 73-93, 73d Cong., February 15, 1934.

38. Arthur Schlesinger, Jr., *The Politics of Upheaval* (Boston: Houghton Mifflin Co., 1960), p. 355.

39. Stanley High, *Roosevelt—And Then?* (New York: Harper and Brothers, 1937), p. 138.

40. Phillips, *Crash to Blitz*, p. 277.

41. Sherwood, *Roosevelt and Hopkins*, p. 68.

42. Letters, James Farley to Harry Hopkins, September 20, 1936 and October 5, 1936, Hopkins MSS, Hyde Park Collection.

43. Thomas E. Dewey, *The Case Against the New Deal* (New York: Harper and Brothers, 1940), pp. 87-96.

44. See Thomas L. Stokes, "Senate Group Gets More Data on WPA—Kentucky Politics," *Washington Daily News*, November 29, 1938, p. 11. For a full account of alleged WPA scandals see the published hearings of the House Un-American Activities Committee, 1937-39; for the Administration's refutations of these attacks, see Press Release Folder, WPA Files, Library of Congress.

45. Raymond Clapper, "Who Is Hopkins?" *Forum* (December 1937), pp. 283-87.

46. Sherwood, *Roosevelt and Hopkins*, p. 92.

47. Raymond Moley, *27 Masters of Politics* (New York: Funk and Wagnalls Co., 1949), p. 41.

48. Interview with Samuel I. Rosenman, April 1, 1970.

49. Oral History Research Office, Columbia University, Arthur Krock MSS, pp. 66-67.

50. Interview with Rosenman, *ibid.*

51. Macmahon, Millett and Ogden, *Federal Work Relief*, p. 190.

8. Presidential Adviser

The Relationship

MUCH HAS BEEN WRITTEN about Harry Hopkins' role as resident White House adviser to the President during the wartime years. [1] This is entirely understandable because during those crucial years and up to the Nixon era, as Anderson has suggested, Hopkins "was probably the most powerful presidential aide who ever lived." [2] Operating almost as a "residential state department" for the President, Hopkins was never further away from the Chief Executive than the length of the corridor which linked their bedrooms in the White House. As Samuel I. Rosenman observes,

> No matter what his official position is—if he's the first person who sees the President in the morning and the last person who sees him at night—he is the second most powerful man in Washington. [3]

During the earlier war years, Hopkins was just such a man in the life of the President.

Less is known and little is understood, however, about the nature of the relationship between Roosevelt and Hopkins during the 1930s. It now becomes apparent that Hopkins played an important role as an adviser to

Roosevelt during this period, especially from 1936 to 1938 when Hopkins' primary position was WPA Administrator.

The explanation for the growing importance of Hopkins' advisory relationship to Roosevelt after 1936 seems to be threefold. First, after the 1936 presidential elections, Roosevelt realized that the WPA was not the political liability that Ickes (and many others) had feared. The solid election showing convinced Roosevelt and Hopkins, if not all Democratic leaders, that the more liberal policies of 1935 and 1936 had the support of the people. This fact cemented the relationship between Hopkins and Roosevelt; fond as he was of Hopkins, the President was too much the politician to stay close to someone who was a political liability. Second, Roosevelt was impressed by the growing political sophistication and effectiveness which Hopkins had shown in the 1936 campaign. The President had received surprisingly favorable reports on Hopkins' performance during the Western campaign swing which the WPA Administrator had made in late summer. Even Jim Farley, the master politician and social work skeptic, had spoken of Hopkins' political effectiveness with warmth and admiration. Finally, Roosevelt lost the services of his most trusted friend Louis Howe, only months before the 1936 election. Hopkins could not be expected to fill this void in Roosevelt's life, for Howe and Hopkins were very different men; nevertheless, the presidency is a lonely job and, as Roosevelt was to tell Wendell Willkie years later, you "discover the need for somebody like Harry Hopkins who asks for nothing except to serve you." [4]

The Men

At first thought, Roosevelt and Hopkins appear to be a portrait in extremes. The President, born to a famous family and the privileges that wealth can bring, was as far from a working-class background as one could be. Hopkins had been brought up in public schools on the Iowa plains; Roosevelt, educated in the elite eastern private schools, reserved for the rich and patrician. However, much as their family birthright differed, their political heritage was essentially the same. Both men shared a political philosophy rooted in Jeffersonian Democracy, the Progressivism of Theodore Roosevelt, and the New Freedom of Woodrow Wilson. From this spirit grew a common trait: a *will* to assume primary responsibility for events, and a *will* to make decisions regarding them. [5]

The nature of the relationship between the two men was very special. Many New Dealers, Raymond Clapper relates, bored Roosevelt with their solemn earnestness—but Hopkins never did. Hopkins knew instinctively when to ask questions and when to keep still, when to approach Roosevelt directly and when to approach from an angle. "Quick, alert, shrewd, bold, and carrying it off with a bright Hell's bells air, Hopkins [became] in all respects the inevitable favorite." [6] "He was as thoroughly Roosevelt's man as anybody in government," adds Paul Appleby,

> but at the same time he was one who fought with the President and fought without gloves. He fought roughly and hard and he argued hard. I think that is the thing that puts the country most in his debt. That's a very useful function, and that's a thing very few people do. [7]

Donald Richberg agrees, noting that Roosevelt enjoyed and trusted "working with a man who might argue freely as to what should be done and how to do it, but who, when a decision was once made, would work with might and main

to carry out the President's program in the way in which
he wanted it carried out." [8] Marquis Childs, usually a
reliable observer, goes a bit further. He suggests that if
Roosevelt had told Hopkins to jump off the Washington
Monument, "the appointed hour would find Mr. Hopkins
poised for the plunge." [9] Even discounting for poetic
hyperbole, Childs seems to miss the essence of their unique
relationship by implying a servility in Hopkins that just
was not present.

As Frances Perkins has noted, the President admired
Hopkins and

> . . . did not look on Hopkins as a relief adminis-
> trator exclusively. He regarded him as a man who
> knew a lot about human nature, who was an ex-
> ceptionally good executive, and whose judgment
> was good on almost any question. [10]

Roosevelt trusted his decisions, and knew Hopkins got
things done. The President therefore gave Hopkins many
time-consuming additional assignments, so that the winter
of 1933-34, for example, found Hopkins as Administrator
of both the FERA and the CWA, and Chairman of the
Federal Surplus Relief Corporation. In the following two
years, Roosevelt appointed his relief administrator to the
President's Drought Committee, National Emergency Council, National Resources Planning Board, and the Committee
on Economic Security.

The Adviser in Action

Perhaps the most important example of Hopkins' role as
an influential presidential adviser during the decade of the
1930s revolves around Roosevelt's change in economic

position in 1938. Rexford Tugwell, himself an economist
and influential Brains Trust member, notes that it was
Hopkins who finally brought about the President's conversion to Keynesianism. Roosevelt tended to be very conservative in economics and his fiscal orthodoxy had been
formidable. As late as 1938, he still believed in the
paramount importance of the sound dollar and the balanced
budget. It was Hopkins, Tugwell asserts, along with Federal
Reserve Chairman Marriner Eccles, who persuaded Roosevelt to embrace deficit spending. [11]

Eccles tells the story:

> Harry Hopkins, who had been most active in earlier
> months in urging a resumption of deficit spending,
> was in Florida at this time [March 1938] recuper-
> ating. . . . While there, he seemed to sense that if he
> once again pressed the President for action . . . he
> might get a favorable answer.

Hopkins and his aides then quickly worked out on paper
the whole case for planned deficit spending. Eccles con-
tinues:

> Armed with this memorandum, Hopkins proceeded
> to Warm Springs. . . . By April 2nd, when the
> presidential train was headed back to Washington,
> with Hopkins aboard, the whole of the budget-
> balancing program had been scrapped. [12]

This was the first time in Roosevelt's five years as President,
notes Tugwell, "that he appeared to have accepted, not
only theoretically but as a matter of positive governmental
virtue, the management of income and outgo as regulator
of the economy." "This genuine conversion," Tugwell
adds, "can be credited to Harry Hopkins as much as to

anyone." [13] Thus is one bold stroke, Hopkins—the man whom many have called a doer but not a thinker—helped in a modest way to shape the future of monetary policy for the nation. As a result, Keynesian deficit spending has continued to influence fiscal planning for the country in both Democratic and Republican administrations.

Power by Appointment

It is one of the interesting characteristics of our political system that a man like Harry Hopkins could have so much influence yet never stand for election. Indeed, he had not been elected to anything since he became class president in his senior year at college. Hopkins illustrates the fact that men who have the trust and respect of elected leaders can shape the destiny of the country in ways that men elected to lesser positions seldom can.

As a presidential adviser in these early years, Hopkins did much to change the policies of the country through his ever-deepening relationship with Roosevelt. Sometimes it was in a single bold stroke, such as the conversion to deficit spending; but, more often than not, it was in little ways that never made the headlines. It would be Hopkins acting as a listening-post for the President through his own network of regional offices, field staff and personal contacts, or Hopkins warning Roosevelt of the unanticipated political consequences of a pending decision—based on his travels throughout the country and his reliable political acumen. The responsibility inherent in the role of presidential adviser, therefore, can be equal to the burden of program administration.

The record of Harry Hopkins is remarkable in that he was both an administrator *and* a presidential adviser in these crucial years, and, most important, that he acquitted himself well in both positions.

1. For the most authoritative study see Sherwood, *Roosevelt and Hopkins;* also see "The Man Who Came to Dinner: Hopkins" in Anderson, *Presidents' Men,* pp. 66-85; and "Lord Root of the Matter: Harry Hopkins" in Louis W. Koenig, *The Invisible Presidency* (New York: Rinehart and Co., Inc., 1960), pp. 299-337.

2. Anderson, *Presidents' Men,* p. 7.

3. Interview with Samuel I. Rosenman, April 1, 1970.

4. Sherwood, *Roosevelt and Hopkins,* p. 3.

5. Grace G. Tully, *F.D.R., My Boss* (New York: Charles Scribner's Sons, 1949), p. 66.

6. Quoted in Sherwood, *Roosevelt and Hopkins,* p. 2.

7. Oral History Research Office, Columbia University, Paul Appleby MSS, p. 156.

8. Donald R. Richberg, *My Hero* (New York: G. P. Putnam's Sons, 1954), p. 241.

9. Childs, "President's Best Friend," *Saturday Evening Post,* April 19, 1941, p. 9.

10. Frances Perkins, *The Roosevelt I Knew* (New York: Viking Press, 1946), pp. 190-91.

11. Tugwell, *Democratic Roosevelt,* pp. 326-28.

12. Marriner S. Eccles, *Beckoning Frontiers,* ed. by Sidney Hyman (New York: Alfred A. Knopf, Inc., 1951), p. 311.

13. Tugwell, *Democratic Roosevelt,* p. 449.

9. What Manner of Man

The Setting

MOST MEN in great positions in Washington could be spotted by their upright personal bearing and the splendor of their office. In a sense, the distinguished stature of the man made the office; in turn, the polished finery of the setting served to make the man. Not so with Harry Hopkins.

Tucked away in the ancient Walker-Johnson building, Hopkins' own office was no larger than a room in a decent hotel. It was dark and untidy, with a potpourri of some of the most undistinguished government furniture in town. The doors were warped, the paint was peeling from the ceiling and walls; and one could not help noticing a pervasive odor of insecticide used in a losing battle against an indomitable population of cockroaches. [1]   Ernie Pyle apostrophized:

> . . . that old office of yours, Mr. Hopkins, good Lord, it's terrible. It's so little in the first place, and the walls are faded and water pipes run up the walls, and your desk doesn't even shine. But I guess you don't care. Maybe it wouldn't look right for you to have a nice office anyway, when you're dealing in misery all the time. [2]

Pyle was right. Hopkins did not care any more about the appearance of his office than about the appearance of his person. Washington, he concluded, was full of people who did, and he was not going to be one of them.

In person, he was tall, wiry and always a little bit disheveled—as if he had slept in his suit the night before. When he talked, his face would appear wry and twisted, his eyes darting left and right, as if he were just a little bit suspicious. He had a generally plain and undistinguished demeanor, and almost anyone who met him agreed that he certainly did not look like anybody special. As Ernie Pyle said:

> And you, Mr. Hopkins, I like you because you look like common people. I don't mean any slur by that either, because they don't come any commoner than I am, but you sit there so easy swinging back and forth in your swivel chair, in your blue suit and blue shirt, and your neck is sort of skinny, like poor people's necks, and you act honest too. [3]

His manner was brusque, outspoken, almost deliberately rude. General Hugh Johnson, an apt phrasemaker and head of the National Recovery Administration (NRA), is quoted as saying that Hopkins "has a mind like a razor, a tongue like a skinning knife, a temper like a Tartar and a sufficient vocabulary of parlor profanity—words kosher enough to get by the censor but acid enough to make a mule-skinner jealous." [4]

Called a whippersnapper and thoroughly ungentlemanly by many of his administrative colleagues, Hopkins confessed:

> There are two kinds of administrators—gentlemen

and go-getters. When a gentleman learns that his appropriation is being cut by the bureau of the budget, he accepts it. But I'm no gentleman. If my appropriation is ever cut, I simply call up the White House and ask the President to issue a stop order, saying that I will go over in a few days and explain why. Then I never go over. That is how a go-getter always beats a gentleman. [5]

In a way, his aggressivenesses and pervasive cynicism were an appropriate counterbalance to his social work idealism. The blend was a useful one. Said Joseph E. Davies, "He had the purity of St. Francis of Assisi combined with the sharp shrewdness of a race track tout." [6]

His Critics

Not all observers were so generous. Not only did his un-bureaucratic iconoclasm infuriate many Washington veterans; they grew to distrust his motives as well. He was alternatively called a Svengali, Machiavelli and Rasputin. [7] "He is a believer in ends before means, a heretic hunter, an 'enthusiast' in the eighteenth-century sense of the word," wrote Alsop and Kintner. [8]   Prominent newspapers began to refer to Hopkins as a Communist, Socialist, Bolshevik, American Caesar and Czar. The *Chicago Daily Tribune* editorial of April 17, 1936 concluded:

Mr. Hopkins is a bull-headed man whose high place in the New Deal was won by his ability to waste more money in quicker time on more absurd undertakings than any other mischievous wit in Washington could think of.

Other critics took a milder and far more subtle approach toward Hopkins, indicating in their critique of his abilities and performance that, after all, he was only a social worker. Thus *Fortune* described him as "the charitarian who has no theories about charity." [9] In a similarly deprecatory manner, Raymond Moley writes:

> Hopkins combined vigorous dispatch in distributing the funds entrusted to him with unorthodox, not to say radical, political and social ideas, most of which were derived from the emotional impact he had experienced in dealing with the poor and unfortunate in his social work. There was never any evidence that he had studied these questions in any depth. [10]

In this way, Hopkins is dismissed as a benevolent anomaly, without depth or theoretical understanding, giving alms with a vigor born of emotional persuasions. Such condescension does not do justice to Hopkins, nor does it appear to be based wholly in fact. While Hopkins was not an academician in the style of Professors Tugwell and Moley, he nevertheless was a philosopher as well as a practitioner, a "thinker" and also a "doer." The quality of Hopkins' own commitment was often mistaken for emotionalism; his pragmatism frequently was misinterpreted as an aversion to (or even incapacity for) reflective, conceptual thinking.

Churchill and Hopkins

It is interesting that one of Hopkins' greatest admirers was the learned and perceptive Sir Winston Churchill. The story of their relationship is one of compatibility and mutual respect. Hopkins, Churchill noted, had the personality to make diplomacy human and the ability to make planning sessions successful. In his unpompous, confident, down-to-earth manner, Hopkins would absorb the facts of a problem, review the historical precedents, weigh the relevant theories, and immediately announce the alternative decisions. After Hopkins died, Churchill wrote to his widow:

> I have been present at several great conferences where twenty or more of the most important executive personages were gathered together. When all discussion flagged and all seemed baffled, it was on these occasions Harry Hopkins would rap out a deadly question: "Surely, Mr. President, here is the point we have got to settle. Are we going to face it or not?"
>
> Faced it always was and being faced, was conquered. [11]

Churchill told Hopkins that if England were to give him a title of nobility, he would suggest Hopkins be dubbed "Lord Root of the Matter" for his ability to pierce to the heart of any problem. Call it what one may—practical or conceptual—it was this quality of thinking that Hopkins brought to his work, and few would question that it proved enormously successful in meeting the unprecedented social problems of the 1930s.

Hopkins and His Staff

Hopkins had a remarkable relationship with his subordinates largely because he viewed them as colleagues. His relationship with his staff was warm and receptive, sympathetic and supporting. Being a thoroughly unpretentious man, Hopkins was candid and receptive. Lorena Hickok, the brilliant newspaper woman who became Hopkins' Chief

Field Investigator for the FERA and WPA, recalls Hopkins'
remarks to her when she was being hired in 1933:

> What I want you to do is to go out around the
> country and look this thing over. I don't want sta-
> tistics from you. I don't want the social worker
> angle. I just want your own reaction as an ordinary
> citizen. Go talk with preachers and teachers, busi-
> nessmen, workers, farmers. Go talk with the un-
> employed, those who are on relief and those who
> aren't, and when you talk with them don't ever for-
> get that but for the grace of God you, I, any of our
> friends might be in their shoes. Tell me what you
> see and hear. All of it. Don't ever pull your
> punches. [12]

This empathy and frankness endeared Hopkins to colleagues
and staff, and the highest caliber personnel came to Washington specifically to work with him. He delegated well and
had a remarkable sense of the equalitarian in his attitude
toward staff and program participants. In a speech in Los
Angeles, he declared:

> I am getting sick and tired of these people on the
> WPA and local relief rolls being called chiselers and
> cheats. It doesn't do any good to call these people
> names, because they are just like the rest of us.
> They don't drink any more than the rest of us, they
> don't lie any more, they're no lazier than the rest of
> us—they're pretty much a cross section of the
> American people....[13]

As a result, he gained the respect and loyalty of his workers.
One of Hopkins' top assistants told Stanley High that most
of the WPA employees were such individualists that other

administrators wondered how Hopkins managed. His explanation was simple: "Most of us here at WPA wouldn't cross the street on orders of WPA. But on an order from Hopkins—if he signed it himself—we'd all with one accord jump out of this seventh-story window." [14]

A Portrait

This man would serve more people directly and spend more public money than anyone to date in American history. In doing so, he would make a total commitment to his job—which to Hopkins meant an unswerving loyalty to the one-third of the nation at the very bottom of the ladder. Once he was asked—after he had left relief work to join the war effort—what single accolade or tribute had meant the most to him during his years with the alphabet agencies he directed. The questioner expected the typical: the testimonials, the recognition by Roosevelt, the honorary degrees. But Hopkins said it was a political cartoon from the *Parkway Transcript* of Roslindale, Massachusetts. Captioned "A Great Record," it showed a simple plaque which read:

To the Everlasting Honor of Harry L. Hopkins
An American boy from Iowa who spent
9 Billions of his country's money
and not a dollar stuck to his fingers! [15]

It was true. The man who spent nine billion dollars died as he had lived, virtually penniless—which is a tribute in the era of Watergate. But, as we shall see, Hopkins' contribution went far beyond his integrity as a public administrator, to include the introduction of a new model for the role of government in the sphere of social welfare. Therein lay his primary impact as a public servant.

NOTES

1. Phillips, *Crash to Blitz,* pp. 265-66.
2. Ernie Pyle, "Hopkins and Ickes Are Quite a Couple of Fellows in Real Life," *Washington News,* October 26, 1935.
3. *Ibid.*
4. Quoted in Edward Robb Ellis, *A Nation in Torment: The Great Depression 1929-1939* (New York: Coward-McCann, 1970), p. 493.
5. Schlesinger, *Politics of Upheaval,* p. 352.
6. William E. Leuchtenburg, *Franklin D. Roosevelt and the New Deal, 1932-1940* (New York: Harper and Row, 1963), p. 120.
7. *Svengali,* a fictional character from du Maurier's "Trilby" was a middle-aged hypnotist and musician with a thin bony face, sallow complexion and piercing eyes. He was considered conceited and generally malicious, alternatively bullying and fawning to gain his objectives. *Machiavelli,* an Italian statesman and author of "The Prince," was popularly considered a cynical and unscrupulous broker of political power. *Rasputin,* a Russian religious adventurer and politician, was considered an evil genius who secretly dominated the government of Czar Nicholas II through his influence in high places and his ability to trade in political favors and appointments.
8. Joseph Alsop and Robert Kintner, *Men Around the President* (New York: Doubleday, Doran and Co., 1939), p. 45. For a scathing (but somewhat factually loose) criticism of Hopkins see John T. Flynn, "Harry the Hop and the Happy Hot Dogs" in *The Roosevelt Myth* (New York: The Devin-Adair Co., 1956), pp. 128-48.
9. "Harry Hopkins," *Fortune Magazine,* XII (July 1935), p. 59.
10. Moley, *First New Deal,* p. 271.
11. Sherwood, *Roosevelt and Hopkins,* p. 5.
12. Letter, Lorena Hickok to Mrs. Godwin (secretary to Hopkins), November 21, 1936, Hickok File, Hopkins MSS, Hyde Park Collection. (This passage is from the manuscript of an introductory chapter for a book which Miss Hickok had in preparation, but never completed.)
13. Sherwood, *Roosevelt and Hopkins,* pp. 83-84. Later Hopkins added, "I believe people are poor, in the main, because we don't know how to distribute the wealth properly." See Ellis, *A Nation in Torment: The Great American Depression, 1929-1939,* p. 490.
14. High, *Roosevelt—and Then?,* p. 134.
15. Newspaper File, Hopkins MSS, Hyde Park Collection.

Part IV

IMPACT OF A PUBLIC SERVANT

"Will you tell me which way I ought to go from here?" said Alice. "That depends on where you want to get to," said the Cat.

Lewis Carroll,
Alice's Adventures in Wonderland

10. Hopkins and the Social Work Profession

The Decade of the 1920s

IN THE 1920s, social workers were engaged mainly in the private sector of social welfare. Thus, it is not surprising that most of them—while more aware than others of the proportions that unemployment was assuming—felt that the voluntary local agencies could respond adequately to the service needs of the people. Most social workers supported President Hoover's campaign of "Mobilizing for Human Need" as a welcome indication of confidence in the ability of private agencies to handle the crisis. In addition, such national campaigns always helped to fill community chests— which provided the lifeblood of private social welfare.

As Nels Anderson relates, in general, social workers "believed, with the leaders of business, that the existing social order was functioning well enough, and while admitting the volume of unemployment, they were unable to look beyond the idle worker for the causes of his idleness." [1] Social workers, like almost everyone else, were influenced deeply by the events and mood of the decade; they were optimistic, little oriented toward social action, and generally pleased with the tenor of laissez-faire. Added to this, of course, was the impact of Freud's theories on social work practice, which deflected questioning of outside forces, and tended to draw one's perspective inward when seeking causes of an individual's plight.

There were a few social work leaders who continued to question Hoover's policies, advocating a policy of political action—among them, Jane Addams, Karl de Schweinitz and Harry Lurie—but an examination of the *Proceedings* of the National Conference of Social Work (NCSW) from the late 1920s through 1931 shows that they were distinctly a minority within the profession. [2]   The majority agreed with Miriam van Waters who said, "We do not plan to build communities, rather we are adjustors, maybe the ameliorators, or we just dodge the traffic." [3]   Even at the NCSW annual meeting in 1931, when there were over six million unemployed, the dominant voice was in favor of strictly local and voluntary programs of relief. There were exceptions to the general rule—notably Jacob Billikopf and Harry Lurie—but the participants refused to endorse the principle of federally supported relief for the unemployed. Typically, the Conference President-elect, C.M. Bookman (director of the Community Chest in Cincinnati), said to the assembly: "I do not believe it will be necessary to make or take national or state grants for direct relief." [4]

In one of the first major statements by a social work leader to call for federal aid, Harry Lurie told the Massachusetts State Conference of Social Work on September 25, 1931:

> It is my opinion that the President has failed utterly in employing the potential powers of the federal government for dealing adequately with the relief aspects of the present emergency. Indeed he has been the chief opponent of measures which would involve the government in a direct program of relief....

He continued to hit hard, concluding that

> an intelligently conceived and executed plan of
> federal aid would be an extremely helpful adjunct
> to the present program of national coordination and
> planning in unemployment relief. [5]

Two months later, New York State would respond with
the first state program of relief, the TERA, and would bring
Harry Hopkins from the voluntary social work sector to
serve as its Executive Director. Then gradually, early in
1932, other states would follow New York's example by
establishing their own relief organizations rather than wait
in vain for action from Hoover. By the time of the 1932
meeting of the National Conference of Social Work, the
tone had changed. While the unemployment problem was
worse, the significant factor seemed to be that Governor
Roosevelt had taken the initiative and others had followed.
At least *state* government intervention in relief was now a
fait accompli, and therefore it had become increasingly
difficult to deny the realities of the problem.

In his outgoing NCSW presidential address, C.M. Bookman reversed his 1931 position. He said the time had come
to recognize that private agencies and local governments
both were overwhelmed. He recommended to social work
leaders at the Conference that state and federal governments enter the picture to shoulder the load. No one, he
argued, could afford to be frightened any longer by the
concept of a "dole." [16] All the while, of course, Roosevelt and Hopkins had been doing for over six months what
the Conference leaders were now recommending to the
rest of the nation.

When Roosevelt became President, social work leaders
took an active part in fighting for passage of the Federal
Emergency Relief Act legislation. Their commitment now

had become complete and sincere. Differences would occur between Hopkins and some social work leaders in the future, however, because the profession tended to see the federal government as giving a blank check for a permanent program of social casework under public auspices. Hopkins made it quite clear in these instances that the FERA funds were for relief of the unemployed—"and not for a number of other perfectly fine and worthy social objectives"—and that a permanent program of relief was not implied by the legislation. [7]   From that point on, social workers could be counted on to follow Hopkins' lead, and to initiate some outstanding suggestions for the future.

Adaptation to Change

The emphasis in social work (which then was principally social casework) had been on the individual in need of adjustment rather than on the adverse effects of the environment upon the individual. Mary Richmond's classic definition of casework in 1922 still obtained. "Social case work," she wrote, "consists of those processes which develop personality through adjustments consciously effected individual by individual, between men and their social environment." [8]

The social welfare practices of the FERA, however, were serving to cement and validate a new, democratic approach to people that began to emerge in the more progressive schools and agencies in the late 1920s. This new philosophy was articulated by Virginia Robinson in 1930:

> The case work relationship is a reciprocal relationship in which the case worker must accept herself and the other equally, in which all of her attitudes toward the client would be such that she would be

content to be at the other end of such a relationship herself. [9]

One is reminded of Hopkins' statement to Lorena Hickok in 1933, quoted earlier: "Go talk with the unemployed, those who are on relief and those who aren't, and when you talk with them don't ever forget that but for the grace of God you, I, any of our friends might be in their shoes." It was no longer possible for the social worker to see himself as an "adjuster of personalities"; the intervention of government had been an admission that all of the fault no longer lay within the individual, and that Freudian psychology could not provide all the answers. Fresh from the experience and ideology of the 1920s, social workers often found it difficult to adjust to an "other-directed" approach and to the democratic concept of social work practice. Many still viewed the unemployed man as requiring "casework techniques" and "therapeutic treatment." But Hopkins was firm in his position. "There could be little doubt," he wrote, "that what most of them needed was not casework, but a job." [10] Or, as E. Wight Bakke wrote, "The primary need of the unemployed was the lack of money, not lack of character, employability or adequate adjustment to community life." [11]   Still another professional, Antoinette Cannon, commenting in a social work journal in 1933, concluded:

> Now, when all persons, strong as well as weak, are either fallen or threatened, when nobody knows what day his turn on the bread-line will come, attention is forcibly directed to the dependence of every person upon the network of social relations within which he lives. [12]

Hopkins translated this new democratic, nonjudgmental

philosophy of social work into a statement to all FERA offices around the country. He pointed out that the administration of unemployment relief was a form of social work which used certain methods of social casework, but was not identical with it, as the term commonly was understood. Social work in the FERA was directed toward a problem which was society's own, outside of the individual and beyond his control. It would be administered, therefore, according to essentially democratic principles and with utmost respect for the dignity and worth of the applicants. [13] In this manner, the new, democratic concept of social work became a nationwide practice of the profession.

Exit Poor Law

As Josephine Brown has noted, the administration of unemployment relief under the FERA marked an epochal turning point in social work philosophy and practice. Not only was the responsibility of government established once and for all; public relief now was recognized as a *right* of people in need, and their worth and dignity as human beings were to be respected. [14] To many people there seemed something almost perverse and un-American about this new approach. They would ask: should we not test for sobriety, thrift and worthiness? Hopkins said "no." He would not patronize recipients, nor would he examine their character and morals, thrift or virtue. "Hopkins did not like to see money wasted," Searle Charles points out. "He was, however, one who believed that a glass of beer probably tasted as good to a man who handled a shovel all day as a cocktail did to those of the local country club set." [15] Some of the Poor Law philosophy was beginning to crumble.

Hopkins also insisted on adequate amounts of relief, rather than marginal doles for subsistence. There was no question that he abjured the doctrine of "less eligibility," [16] and wanted to make relief as adequate as possible. Great pressure was brought to bear on state and local officials who were still influenced by the Poor Law philosophy. "The Federal Relief Administration does not intend to subsidize miserably low wages," said Hopkins. "We do not intend to permit anybody to use relief funds to reduce the standard of living lower than it is now. We are not going to allow relief agencies to starve people slowly to death with our money." [17] Later, Hopkins was to write that the government never did give adequate relief, even with the best of intentions. But, in speaking of FERA relief recipients he added, "We can only say that out of every dollar entrusted to us for the lessening of their distress, the maximum amount humanly possible was put into their hands." [18] Even more important than the dollar figures, however, was the philosophy that Hopkins brought to social work practice and, in turn, to the country.

A Change in Professional Image

The image of social workers before the Depression was that of gatekeeper for society. They were known for industry, courage, dedication and integrity—a bulwark against nepotism and spoils. With the advent of the FERA, they were needed in great number to protect the public purse by investigating families who claimed an eligibility for relief. As Josephine Brown points out,

> social workers carried the onus which comes from standing at the point of intake, for they performed the difficult task of deciding who would or would

not get relief in every city and county Emergency
Relief Administration in the country. [19]

The known professional integrity of social workers was
seen as ensuring an honest, nonpolitical program. They seldom were viewed, however, in terms of their professional
skills and competence. They were merely the guardians of
public morality. With the growth of relief and public work
programs the image began to change. Social workers were
no longer "honest ladies" donating time to a worthy cause,
but rather program administrators and policy makers.
Hopkins described their new roles discerningly:

> There was and is, I know, a certain prejudice
> against social workers, but what does the record
> show? In community after community, where well-
> meaning volunteers had been handling relief, we
> cut costs in half by installing a trained social service
> personnel. The "professionals" paid for themselves
> a hundred times over. [20]

The adjustment to new and increased responsibilities
was not always easy, even for some of the most highly
trained workers, for they had been prepared to deal with
individuals in the one-to-one casework relationship. Frequently, there had been little in their professional education or experience to prepare them for administrative work
per se. But it is a matter of record that, by and large, social
workers acquitted themselves well in their new positions
of responsibility.

With their new roles came public acceptance of a new
image. An editorial in *Public Management* noted this
change:

> To many officials social work, a few years ago,

meant dispensing relief through the local private charity; and in the minds of some officials, the larger task of providing shelter, food and other essentials for thousands of law-abiding citizens is still confused with this earlier experience.

But consider the complicated problems of the confused families and individuals who are victims of this [Depression] phenomenon. Are these problems so simple that anybody can do the job? Isn't it time that those with training and experience in good social welfare techniques be put on this job and well-wishers or political charity mongers be sent to the benches?...[21]

The "charity mongers" *were* "sent to the benches," and social work became an accepted function in government. Social workers, in turn, took on new responsibilities which were qualitatively different as well as quantitatively greater.

Education for Practice

Harry Hopkins had been very active in professional aspects of social work during his earlier career; in fact, he had been chairman of the committee which produced the "Providence Resolutions" in 1920 that provided the philosophical basis for forming the American Association of Social Workers. Like many social workers of that era, however, he never had gone to a social work school for professional training; indeed, Hopkins had never attended any graduate school. He had a benevolent, if not somewhat cavalier attitude toward graduate social work education while, at the same time, understanding the central importance of professional preparation for practice. Typically, when Elizabeth Wisner told Hopkins she was leaving the Red Cross staff to go to social work school, Hopkins remarked, "Oh, you want the laying on of hands!" [22]

In spite of this attitude, Hopkins took a firm stand on the need for expanding social work training, supporting his intentions with a plan and money. Early in 1934 he earmarked approximately $420,000 to be allotted to states exclusively for sending their relief workers to accredited schools of social work for professional preparation. As a result, during the 1934-35 academic year, 912 persons (selected from the staffs of the relief administrations of thirty-nine states) were thus enabled by the FERA to matriculate as students in twenty-one different schools of social work. (The nine states omitted from the grants were states which were thought to have made adequate provision for themselves.) The state administrations, stimulated by the federal example, sent another 225 students to twelve schools for training. These 1,137 students were able to attend for part of an academic year only, and therefore could not complete degree requirements; but, as Sophonisba Breckinridge notes, "they matriculated, and for a period of time were full-time students in a program of professional education, generally on a graduate as well as a professional level. The implications of this statesmanlike action of the FERA," she suggests, "are worth considering." [23]

Attracted by obvious new manpower needs and the lure of public funds, many colleges were anxious to establish new social work curriculums or special (i.e., segregated) programs for FERA students. Unprofessional entrepreneurs were eager to become involved, and many set up unrecognized "institutes" to provide "crash" training programs (even by correspondence courses!), in order to receive federal funds. The FERA rejected all of these alternatives and took a firm stand on financing fellowships only to accredited graduate schools of social work. This decision was crucial in strengthening the professional base of social work nationally, and in helping the accredited institutions improve the quality and diversity of their training. In addition, by working through the American Association of Social Workers and the American Association of Schools of Social Work, the FERA gave responsibility and recognition to these two relatively young professional organizations— both of which would play a significant role in the future development, expansion and professionalization of social work as a respected discipline. [24]

Stimulus to the Profession

There can be little question that the appointment of Harry Hopkins to administer the FERA brought new stature and recognition to social work in America. Indeed, the fact that a social worker was chosen to head the nation's first program of public relief was so important that one must conjecture as to what the state of the social work profession today would be if, for example, a businessman or economist had been chosen instead. The appointment was not only an elevation of Hopkins, but of social work as well. "Congratulations on your appointment as Federal Relief Administrator," said Aubrey Williams in a telegram to Hopkins. "By the quality of your technical and executive service in New York State you have placed professional social work in line for this signal recognition..." [25] In effect, the President had given support to the principle that the administration of relief was a social work function.

The situation was remarkable when viewed in an historical perspective. At the time of Hopkins' appointment to administer the FERA, social work was in its relatively early stages of professional development. The American Association of Schools of Social Work and the American Association of Social Workers were only fourteen and twelve years old, respectively. The first graduate curriculum had been prescribed only the year before (1932), and no firm standards for membership and admission of schools to these organizations had as yet been established. In fact, Abraham Flexner in 1915 had told the National Conference of Social Work that the field was an "occupation" but not a profession; and, as late as 1937, Grace Marcus—a respected social work leader—concluded that social work still was "not yet" a profession. [26]

Whether public relief would have been a social work function if Hopkins had not been selected as administrator can never be known, but we do know that his appointment brought about a demand for social workers almost overnight around the nation. For the first time in the history of social work, a federal agency possessed and was willing to spend large sums of money to employ more social workers than could be found. They were needed as investigators, field representatives, local administrators, interviewers—and to staff the FERA's Social Service Division, which was to prove the exclusive domain of the social work profession.

"I want at least one competent social worker," said Hopkins, "in every district office in America." [27] And thus in one sentence, the die surely had been cast. All over the country, where there never had been the sign of a social worker before, social workers suddenly appeared. "Competent emergency relief organizations," noted Edith Abbott, "with state divisions, regional and district supervisors, and county social work units, have been set up in areas where social-work standards had heretofore barely existed." [28]

The demand created by the FERA brought thousands of young men and women flocking to take social work courses at the colleges and universities. This stimulated the organization of undergraduate curricula, the inception of several new schools of social work, and also a greatly increased attendance at the (then) twenty-eight accredited schools.

Thus it was no coincidence that the number of social workers almost doubled between 1930 and 1940. [29] Many of the new social workers were men, which had an impact on a profession which often had been considered a women's domain. Lending a masculine image to social work in its highest echelons, Hopkins tended to surround himself with such other men in the profession as Robert Kelso, Frank Bane, Aubrey Williams, C. M. Bookman, Sherrard Ewing and Rowland Haynes. The women did not seem to mind. Edith Abbott, Dean at the University of Chicago School of Social Service, complained to Frank Bane about the FERA scholarship program. "I'm getting too many women here....You tell Harry to send me some men and I mean sure enough men. I don't care if they chew tobacco and spit on the floor." [30]

Social Work Goes Public

The argument for giving the new public monies over to the private agencies has been discussed earlier. To many social workers it seemed both logical and desirable. The private field, after all, had the structure, existing organization, trained staff, its own volunteers—and, in many ways, looked like the natural place to turn for help. The public sector, meanwhile, was poorly organized and staffed, thinly financed, and of questionable repute. Referring to the annual National Conference of Social Work, Bane recalls:

> In those days there was a section of the NCSW, Section 9, which was called Public Welfare Officials Section, and it always had the back room....we were regarded if not as politicians, as people who have to handle the day-to-day routine dishwashing jobs....
> [31]

Public welfare before 1933 had meant the administration of relief by irresponsible and usually untrained officials— political hacks, holding down "spoils" jobs.

By interpreting the FERA legislation to mean that public funds should be controlled by nonpartisan public officials, Hopkins built the public sector of social work virtually from scratch. Not only did he build a tradition of public social service—important in itself—he prepared the public sector to receive more and greater responsibility for social welfare programs in the decades to follow. [32]   His decision to funnel money and program through the public sector changed the image and stature of public welfare, and, at the same time, prepared for the institutionalization of public social services throughout the country.

NOTES

1. Nels Anderson, *The Right to Work* (New York: Modern Age Books, 1938), p. 128. Also see Shirley C. Hellenbrand, "Main Currents in Social Casework: 1918-1936" (Unpublished D.S.W. dissertation, Columbia University Press, 1957), Ch. 6.

2. See Frank J. Bruno, *Trends in Social Work: 1874-1956* (New York: Columbia University Press, 1957), Ch. 31.

3. Miriam van Waters, "The New Morality and the Social Worker," in National Conference of Social Work, *Proceedings of the 56th Annual Meeting* (San Francisco, 1929), p. 70.

4. National Conference of Social Work, *Proceedings of the 58th Annual Meeting* (Philadelphia, 1931).

5. Harry L. Lurie, "The Place of Federal Aid in Unemployment Relief," *Social Service Review*, V (December 1931), pp. 524, 535.

6. National Conference of Social Work, *Proceedings of the 59th Annual Meeting* (Chicago, 1932), pp. 3-23.

7. Harry L. Hopkins, "The Developing National Program of Relief," in National Conference of Social Work, *Proceedings of the 60th Annual Meeting* (Detroit, 1933).

8. Mary Richmond, *What Is Social Case Work?* (New York: Russell Sage Foundation, 1922), pp. 98-99.

9. Virginia Robinson, *A Changing Psychology in Social Case Work* (Chapel Hill, N.C.: University of North Carolina Press, 1930), pp. 170-71.

10. Hopkins, *Spending to Save,* pp. 133-34. Hopkins himself was not a trained social worker—he never attended a graduate school—and perhaps this was helpful in freeing him from looking only to psychology for the answer to what were essentially social and economic problems.

11. E. Wight Bakke, quoted in Charles, *Minister of Relief,* p. 23.

12. M. Antoinette Cannon, "Recent Changes in the Philosophy of Social Workers," *The Family,* XIV (October 1933), p. 195.

13. "Social Work in the Administration of Unemployment Relief," April 30, 1935 (mimeographed), FERA Current File, National Archives.

14. Brown, *Public Relief,* p. 229.

15. Charles, *Minister of Relief,* p. 59.

16. This doctrine involved making relief as distasteful as possible by keeping relief grants smaller than the lowest wages which the recipient possibly could earn if work were available.

17. Hopkins, "Developing Program of Relief," *Proceedings of the National Conference of Social Work* (Chicago: University of Chicago Press, 1933).

18. Hopkins, *Spending to Save,* p. 99. One might note that the President of the Reconstruction Finance Corporation said in July 1932: "I have a very high regard for social workers, but God forbid they should have the purse strings." Bernstein, *Lean Years,* p. 470.

19. Brown, *Public Relief,* p. 151.

20. Harry L. Hopkins, "Food for the Hungry," *Collier's,* December 7, 1935, p. 10.

21. Editorial, *Public Management,* XX (March 1938), p. 65.

22. Letter, Elizabeth Wisner to author, March 14, 1970.

23. "The Federal Relief Administration and the Association of Schools of Social Work," typed manuscript dated August 15, 1935 in Papers and Correspondence File, Breckinridge MSS, Library of Congress.

24. See "FERA Training for Social Work," American Association of Schools of Social Work File (1934), Breckinridge MSS, Library of Congress.

25. Telegram, Aubrey Williams to Harry Hopkins, May 20, 1933, Congratulations Folder, FERA Files, National Archives.

26. "The Profession of Social Work," paper presented at the Annual Meeting of the American Association of Schools of Social Work, January 27, 1938, Correspondence File (1938), Breckinridge MSS, Library of Congress. It is remarkable to note, however, the attention which the seventeen-year-old AASW received at the White House. For example, a copy of the Association's "Relief Survey for 1938" (in the Hopkins MSS, Hyde Park Collection) has a hand-written covering memo: "H.H.—will you read and talk to me about this—s/F.D.R."

27. "The Works Program,"Address by Harry L. Hopkins at WPA Field Representatives' Conference, Washington, D.C., December 28, 1935 in *Principal Speeches of Harry L. Hopkins* (Milwaukee, Wisc.: n.p., 1938), p. 3.

28. Edith Abbott, "Don't Do It, Mr. Hopkins!", *The Nation*, January 9, 1935, p. 42.

29. *Social Work Year Book—1945* (New York: American Association of Social Workers, 1945), p. 448.

30. Oral History Research Office, Columbia University, Bane MSS, p. 100.

31. *Ibid.*, p. 94.

32. Hopkins' impact on the social work profession and on the development of public social services, however, has been seriously overlooked by most observers. For example, a scholarly study recently was undertaken on casework and social service delivery in the 1930s, with virtually no mention of Harry Hopkins. Indeed, no notice whatever of Hopkins was made even in a special chapter entitled, "This Business of Relief: The Public Service Solution." See Ann Hartman, "Casework in Crisis: 1932-1941" (unpublished D.S.W. dissertation, Columbia University, 1972), Ch. 6.

II. Hopkins and Public Administration

Historical Perspective

THE ROLE HOPKINS PLAYED in changing the field of public administration can best be understood by examining the central doctrines of public administration that prevailed in 1933. Influenced by the abuses of the late 19th century, concern still was expressed more for political reform than for positive or creative approaches to administration. The tasks of government were divided neatly into two parts, decision and execution, and the role of the administrator was exclusively the latter. Deciding *what* should be done (that is, the shaping of policy) was considered "politics" and, as such, was the exclusive domain of the politician. As Frank Goodnow's early text underscored, public administration had to be separated both from partisan politics and the making of policy. Administrators, it was argued, should tend to the business of carrying out whatever decisions were reached in the political arena. [1] Politics was considered dirty business; professional administrators should content themselves with executing impartial, unquestioning and efficient service in a rational manner. Rationality was possible, they reasoned, because scientific management experts had found certain "fixed principles" of administration which could be followed in decision-making as well as a list of "best ways" to perform the tasks of government. In this manner, administration could become rational, economic, efficient and completely untainted by partisan politics. [2]

This orthodox philosophy fitted quite well with the Harding-Coolidge-Hoover decade of the 1920s. Fixed principles were followed, organizational charts were constructed, economy and efficiency were lauded (always with private enterprise as the model), and bureaucracies were built into every public department. In weighing the impact of Harry Hopkins on the growth and development of public administration, one has to place the practices of his relief agencies in perspective with the conditions which prevailed until his appearance on the federal scene.

Hopkins himself was contemptuous of bureaucratic procedure. In fact, one of his chief concerns was to prevent relief from falling heir to a dull and undiscerning bureaucracy. When inspectors from the Bureau of the Budget came around asking to see his "organizational chart" for the FERA, they were told there wasn't any, as Hopkins would not permit one to be made. "I don't want anybody around here," he said, "to waste any time drawing boxes." [3]

The Positive Approach

As head of the successive relief administrations, Hopkins presided over what then was the largest administrative undertaking in the peacetime history of American government. The key to success, he reasoned, was to set goals as precisely as possible and then move boldly ahead to reach them. "He was more interested in the goal to be gained than in the method by which it was achieved," suggest Macmahon, Millett and Ogden. "This absorption in ends rather than means was truly a quality of leadership." [4] He felt he could not afford the means-end displacement so common in bureaucratic organizations. [5]   A target had to be set and every source at his command pointed in the direction of that goal. If people were going to get in his way with diversions or displacements he would tell them to move aside. "He is a go-getter," remarked the tough-talking NRA director General Hugh Johnson:

> ...He moves across straight lines to his objectives, and if he has a tongue like a scalpel, the skinned usually deserve what they get and more. [6]

Hopkins had a positive approach to administration that took many traditional Washington bureaucrats by surprise. He felt that one could not dodge important decisions by passing them on to "a committee" or "for future consideration" simply because they were controversial. He shared the dilemmas of this approach with Hallie Flanagan when he hired her as theater arts project director for the WPA. "Can you spend money?" he asked. Mrs. Flanagan said somewhat facetiously that the ability to spend money was one of her virtues. But Hopkins continued, seriously:

> It's not easy. It takes a lot of nerve to put your signature down on a piece of paper when it means that the government of the United States is going to pay out a million dollars to the unemployed in Chicago. It takes decision, because you'll have to decide whether Chicago needs that money more than New York City or Los Angeles. You can't care very much what people are going to say because when you're handling other people's money whatever you do is always wrong. If you try to hold down wages, you'll be accused of union-busting and of grinding down the poor; if you pay a decent wage, you'll be competing with private industry

and pampering a lot of no-accounts; if you scrimp
on production costs, they'll say your shows are
lousy and if you spend enough to get a good show
on, they'll say you're wasting the taxpayers' money.
Don't forget that whatever happens you'll be
wrong. [7]

Hopkins showed that an able executive did not have to be
a "yes" man, and this reversed the entrenched attitudes of
the administrations of earlier decades.

Politics and Administration

As we have noted, Hopkins set a remarkable record for
keeping partisan politics and patronage out of the FERA
and CWA programs. When he found Governor Davey of
Ohio, for example, using FERA funds for political purposes
Hopkins assumed direct federal control of the state FERA
program. Governor Davey fought back, evoking, unsuccess-
fully, all kinds of political pressures. Hopkins stood firm,
and when he went to Cleveland soon afterwards to deliver
a speech, he found unsuspected pockets of support. In an
editorial, the *Cleveland Plain Dealer* commented that Hopkins "gives the impression of being a straight hitter as well
as a straight shooter." Most people who met him and heard
him, they concluded, "were satisfied that so far as he con-
trols the expenditures they will be made strictly on
merit." [8]
    He selected his own personnel for the FERA and CWA
with the same disregard for politics. "His main concern
was the zeal and competence of his staff," notes Charles.
"He chose hundreds of men and women solely on the basis
of their ability, experience and knowledge of the problems
of social work and relief." [9]   In 1934, Washington's

"Unofficial Observer" commented:

> Give the Roosevelt Administration a dozen Hop-
> kinses and a few more years and you will see them
> establish a new standard of efficiency in public
> service, a standard comparable to the prewar Ger-
> man public service or to the British Civil Service at
> its best in integrity and immunity to political
> influence. [10]

This did not mean that Hopkins accepted the Goodnow
politics-administration dichotomy in his role as a program
administrator. For while he felt that patronage and nepotism had no place in personnel management, he was convinced that one of the crucial skills of the public administrator was an ability to engage in the political arena to sell
a program to the Congress and to the public.

He was extraordinarily effective with Congress, making
small compromises when demanded without sacrificing the
principal goals of his program. Frances Perkins, herself a
gifted administrator as Secretary of Labor, later wrote of
Hopkins, "He proved to have a natural talent...for those
political adjustments which are so essential to a social
worker carrying out a health and welfare program imping-
ing on public policy." [11]

Hopkins' ability to handle himself from the public plat-
form was equally impressive. During the fall of 1936, he
took an extended trip through the West to explain the WPA
program to the people. If New Deal policies and programs
were to continue, Roosevelt had to be reelected, and it was
Hopkins' responsibility to interpret the Administration's
work relief policies to the public. Some of the reactions
are worth noting. One WPA state director wrote:

> I have not talked with anyone who attended the

luncheon who did not come away thoroughly sold
not only on Mr. Hopkins but upon the program.
From that standpoint the effectiveness of his visit
is particularly outstanding. For example, one of the
newspaper reporters told me that while he had been
in the newspaper business for 14 years he had never
heard anyone who was more impressive and who
did more to destroy any erroneous impressions
which had been created than Mr. Hopkins.... There
has been no national figure, outside of the President,
in Colorado who has demonstrated so much effectiveness as has Mr. Hopkins. [12]

And another added:

I feel that Mr. Hopkins could go into any community in the State of Washington and talk to an
average group of citizens and convince at least
2/3ds of them of the necessity for a works program. In addition, he would impress the remaining
1/3d with the seriousness of the problem involved. [13]

Hopkins continued to develop this art of handling himself
in political situations because he saw it as an essential skill
of an administrator in the public sector.

Staff Supervision

Hopkins developed a style of supervision that was all his
own. Breaking from rules and tradition, he refused to speak
of formal principles in the same fashion that he rejected
the organizational chart. This was but one of his traits that
motivated capable people to work under his leadership.

"Most of the members of this crusading force are exceedingly able," wrote Stanley High. "Most of them work for the WPA, not because they could not get a job anywhere else, but because they like it." [14]   As a result, Hopkins brought scores of highly competent deputies to assist him: social workers, engineers, lawyers, economists and architects. He seemed to attract quality personnel by the example of his commitment and his style as an administrator; and, once staff members became part of the Hopkins' team, they showed intense loyalty to their leader—from bureau chief to messenger. Lt. Col. John Lee, a West Point engineer assigned to study the CWA for the War Department, wrote about Hopkins' relationship with staff, and what they achieved:

> The accomplishments of the CWA were possible through the arduous efforts of the young Administrator and the group of able young assistants he had assembled and inspired. They have worked daily long into the night with a morale easily comparable to that of a war emergency. These assistants address Mr. Hopkins fondly as "Harry." There is no rigidity or formality in their staff conferences with him, yet he holds their respect, confidence and seemingly whole-souled cooperation. [15]

The atmosphere of informality was part of Hopkins' style. Louis Brownlow, an authority in the area of administration, described Hopkins' planning for the CWA with his staff:

> As each suggestion came up, there was discussion free and open; and then, usually by consensus and sometimes, where there was a deep division, by edict, Harry Hopkins made the decision and assigned

the tasks and delegated the work to one of the men in the room. [16]

This was the way Hopkins liked to do business. Because he saw administration as a type of productive interpersonal relations, he avoided memorandums and directives. He believed that there was a creative chemistry in face-to-face relationships, and saw himself as what he truly was—the catalytic agent in the administrative setting. In effect, Hopkins refuted the scientific management school by asserting that administration was a blend of art and science, personality and skill, the expressive and the instrumental.

Hopkins' example tended to be followed by his staff, who generally favored his style and values. They were infected by his enthusiasm and worked arduously. "Hopkins is skilled in getting people to do things," wrote Jonathan Mitchell in *New Republic:*

> If you are aware of the inter-family ear-biting and nose-twisting of other New Deal agencies you can appreciate Hopkins' gift. To an almost comical degree, his associates all have the same duralumin, stream-lined minds, the same filing-case memories, the same boredom in the presence of pomposity, repetitiousness and legalistic obscurity of officialdom. [17]

Education in Administration

Not only did Hopkins and the New Deal agencies for relief attract many capable young people to public administration, they also stimulated an interest in a career with government. Public officials were now looked on increasingly as responsible professionals rather than as political hacks. In the social welfare arena especially, for the first time, a career in public welfare administration became an attractive alternative to serving in the private sector.

The professional schools and associations in social work were already in full swing when the field of public administration was starting to develop as a professional discipline. Until the stimulus of the Brownlow Committee on Administrative Management in the late 1930s, no national organization officially had been formed, and the actual inception of the American Society for Public Administration did not take place until 1939. The major initial responsibility for educating personnel for social welfare administration, therefore, was undertaken by the social work profession. The social work schools began to broaden their curricula to include more emphasis on administration. Gradually, administration became accepted as a partner with casework and groupwork, and in 1959, the Council on Social Work Education's *Curriculum Study* concluded that administration was a full-fledged practice method. [18]

There was considerable feeling, however, that professional preparation for social work and public administration should become a joint enterprise. "The danger," said Florence Sytz in 1936, "is that professional education for social work and public administration may travel separate roads as far as the welfare services of government are concerned.... The immediate problem of this Association [of Social Workers] is to bridge the gap that is developing between social work and public administration." [19] While some graduate programs were sponsored jointly for many years—such as the Graduate School of Public Administration and Social Service at New York University—the marriage proved to be an unnatural one; today most of the preparation for social welfare administration is carried on in separate schools and curricula of both social work and public administration. There can be little question, however, that the attractiveness of the public sector was enhanced by the reputation of the early relief agencies of the 1930s, and for this, Hopkins and his colleagues may take their fair share of the credit.

Federal-City Relations

Perhaps Hopkins' most revolutionary impact on public administration came in the field of federal-city relations. Until the Depression, the subject of federal-city involvement was not considered either important or appropriate. In one of the first textbooks on city government, for example, Goodnow wrote, "As the city has no relations with national government it is not necessary for our purpose that we make any study of the national administrative system." [20]   Cities, after all, were creatures of the sovereign states, and attention of the federal government, it was argued, should be directed toward working with the states themselves as intended in the Constitution.

Federal-city developments began to assume startling significance in 1932, however, due to the desperate financial plight of the urban areas. [21] Necessary expenditures were skyrocketing at a time when sources of revenue were drying up. State budgets were endangered because state credit was unable to stand further strain. The response of the Roosevelt Administration, via the FERA, was a grant-in-aid program to the states. The states, in turn, were responsible for apportioning the money to cities, counties and other political subdivisions.

The innovation in federal-local relations, however, came with the WPA legislation which eschewed the grant-in-aid system in preference for federal control that would permit, for the first time, direct federal-local contacts and funding. Hopkins recognized that the state legislatures, lacking proportional representation, were disproportionately representative of rural interests. In addition, without drastic reform, the state governments would continue to be unable to respond adequately to urban social needs. If the cities were to get a fair share of the WPA funds, Hopkins reasoned, he must be able to deal with them directly.

Experts in intergovernmental relations witnessed the new operating procedure of the WPA with great interest. By 1936, some authorities had grasped the significance:

> There can be no denial that a new pattern of city-federal relations has been woven before our eyes in the past several years. The old charts and diagrams of American government that hung in political science classrooms prior to 1932 have had to be filled in with brand new lines of communication and supply running directly from the federal government to the municipalities.

> Most portentous of all, perhaps, is the renovation and extension of the old system of federal grant-in-aid to the states, which has been familiar in this country since the Morrill Act of 1862. Now, for the first time in American history, cities are the recipients of direct federal benefits without the necessity of having the federal moneys funneled to them through the state governments. [22]

Some foreign commentators (seeing the growth in federal-city relations) suggested that the United States was undergoing a transition from a federal to a unitary state, but, of course, this was not true. [23] Instead, what was taking place was an adaptation which would serve to meet a changing situation in the country without requiring a fundamental alteration of federalism and state sovereignty. The success of this innovation can be measured, in part, by the acceptance coming from both the cities and the states. In effect, what Hopkins had done was to recognize the reality of growing urbanism in the nation, and to devise a solution that would meet this problem, quite unforeseen by our Founding Fathers, in a way that would be politically palatable, and consistent with a need for enlarging the sphere of cooperation among all three levels of government—federal, state and local. "The federal-city relationships which have come into being since 1932," write Betters, Williams and Reeder, "should help to point the way not to federal control over cities, but to a new plane of federal-city cooperation in the complicated business of governing." [24]

Hopkins the Administrator

Hopkins thus made two great contributions to public administration. First, he ushered in a new era of intergovernmental relations. It would be one more realistic, more modern, and in many ways, more flexible than that known before. It would mark the early stages of a continuing quest for a cooperative federalism with federal, state and local governments as working partners.

Second, in style and performance, Hopkins symbolized a break with the traditions of public administration which had held sway during the first two decades of the century. In this sense, he was ahead of his time, rejecting the fixed principles of administration before Gulick and Urwick carefully set them down, and practicing a theory of organizational cooperation several years before Chester Barnard made the notion popularly acceptable. [25] Unorthodox in his style and iconoclastic in his actions, Hopkins broke with the past, charting new directions for public administration which he himself practiced—innovations which would help to reshape the art of government.

1. Frank Goodnow, *Politics and Administration* (New York: The Macmillan Co., 1900).

2. Dwight Waldo, *The Study of Public Administration* (New York: Random House, 1955), Ch. 5; and William F. Willoughby, *Principles of Public Administration* (Baltimore: Johns Hopkins University Press, 1927).

3. Sherwood, *Roosevelt and Hopkins*, p. 49. Hopkins also refused to hire a General Counsel for the FERA, saying, "Lawyers just tell you what you can't do; I'm interested in getting things done."

4. Macmahon, Millett and Ogden, *Federal Work Relief*, p. 190.

5. For a discussion of goal displacement see Robert K. Merton, *Social Theory and Social Structure* (2d ed., Glencoe, Ill.: Free Press, 1957), p. 199.

6. Hugh S. Johnson, *The Blue Eagle: From Egg to Earth* (Garden City, N.Y.: Doubleday, Doran and Co., 1935), p. 426. General Johnson added, "I think he [Hopkins] has done the cleanest-cut job in the whole recovery show."

7. Hallie Flanagan, "WPA Spending," in William E. Leuchtenburg, ed., *The New Deal: A Documentary History* (Columbia, S.C.: University of South Carolina Press, 1968), p. 74.

8. Editorial, *Cleveland Plain Dealer*, May 25, 1935.

9. Charles, *Minister of Relief*, p. 54.

10. [John Franklin Carter], *The New Dealers* (New York: Simon and Schuster, 1934), p. 184.

11. Frances Perkins, "People Mattered to Harry Hopkins," *Survey Midmonthly*, LXXXII (February, 1946), pp. 38-39.

12. Letter, Paul D. Shriver to Robert H. Hinckley, September 29, 1936, Hopkins MSS, Hyde Park Collection.

13. Letter, Don G. Abel to Robert H. Hinckley, October 3, 1936, Hopkins MSS, Hyde Park Collection.

14. High, *Roosevelt—and Then?*, p. 132.

15. John C. Lee, "The Federal Civil Works Administration: A Study Covering Its Organization in November, 1933 and Its Operations Until 31 March 1934," (mimeographed), Hopkins MSS, Hyde Park Collection.

16. Louis Brownlow, *A Passion for Anonymity* (Chicago: University of Chicago Press, 1958), p. 288.

17. Jonathan Mitchell, "Alms-Giver: Harry L. Hopkins," *New Republic*, April 10, 1935, p. 235.

18. See Irving Weissman, ed., *Social Work Curriculum Study* (N.Y.: Council on Social Work Education, 1959), Vols. 3, 7 and 12.

19. Florence Sytz, "Personnel For Social Welfare Services," in *This Business of Relief*, p. 116.

20. Frank J. Goodnow, *City Government in the United States* (New York: Doubleday Co., 1904), p. 69.

21. See Paul V. Betters, *Federal Services to Municipal Governments* (Washington: The Brookings Institution, 1931).

22. Betters, Williams and Reeder, *Federal-City Relations*, p. 136.

23. The example of Germany often was used to bolster the argument. Germany was then a federal state where the cities were forced by a financial crisis to accept fiscal and political domination by the national government. Persons citing this example, however, overlooked the difference between Germany—where all municipal powers could be granted or withheld by unilateral action on the part of the national government—and America, where the Constitution (and 10th Amendment) guarantee a truly federal system. The only way in which the federal government in this country could assume direct control over the cities would be by abolishing the sovereign powers of the several states, and this would mean scrapping much of the Constitution.

24. Betters, Williams and Reeder, *Federal-City Relations,* p. 136.

25. See Chester I. Barnard, *The Functions of the Executive* (Cambridge, Mass.: Harvard University Press, 1939); and Luther Gulick and Lyndall Urwick, *Papers on the Science of Administration* (New York: Institute of Public Administration, 1937).

12. The Legacy of Harry Hopkins

A Nation in Trouble

HOPKINS was neither an economist nor a student of political science. Nevertheless, he understood the dilemma facing the country when Roosevelt came to office. The nation was seriously divided between those who were prospering and those who had no bread for their children. Businessmen kept arguing that the strength of America lay in its confidence in the private enterprise system; and—despite clear evidence that this reliance on the private sector was not working—Hoover continued to express trust in their position. Hopkins saw the fallacy and contradiction. "Predatory business refused to take the responsibility along with the privileges," he wrote. "It did not see that the sovereign people, who gave it so much freedom, were entitled, in return, to a workable economic system—to jobs, continued opportunities, and security. Business, willing to attend to the earning of money and the investment of profits, had little interest in the democratic distribution of income." [1]

The statistics were revealing. In 1926, the Federal Trade Commission reported to the U.S. Senate on national wealth and income. From a representative sampling of the American population, they found that 1% of the people owned about 60% of the wealth, and that 13% of the people owned over 90% of the resources of the country. [2]

The Threat to Democracy

"The fear of revolution," writes David Shannon, "was widespread during the last several months of President Hoover's administration." [3] Confidence in America was at low ebb as people grew restless and hungry. Irving Bernstein gives a vivid account in his study, *The Lean Years:*

> There were "ominous mutterings" in the Southern Appalachian camps. A West Virginia editor told the Red Cross that almost every man in his county had a rifle. Clarence Pickett of the Friends wrote POUR [The Presidents' Organization on Unemployment Relief] of a dangerous possibility of rioting. Crowds were increasingly aggressive. At Hazard, Kentucky, the police were unable to maintain control at the Red Cross food warehouse. "The Negro is not laughing and he is not dancing," Roy Wilkins of the NAACP warned. "The leaders of our organizations," Edward F. McGrady of the AFL told the Senate Manufacturer's Subcommittee, "have been preaching patience....But I say to you gentlemen, advisedly, that if something is not done and starvation is going to continue and perhaps increase, the doors of revolt in this country are going to be thrown open." When Mayor Cermak of Chicago appeared before the House Banking and Currency Committee on June 21, 1932, he said the federal government had a basic choice: relief or troops. [4]

Ernest K. Lindley, an astute observer of the day, reported

that in May 1932, one of Roosevelt's closest friends sum-
marized his own opinion this way. "If Hoover is reelected,"
he predicted, "the chances are at least one in three that
next winter will bring widespread disorders which will grow
into a revolution or be repressed by armed force." [5]

The situation was critical. By March 1933, 15,000,000
Americans had lost their jobs, and the people were increasingly restless. The banking system had collapsed, and
only one month before, Adolf Hitler had seized power in
Germany. On that cold, overcast day on which Roosevelt
was sworn into office, Arthur Schlesinger concludes, the
American experiment in self-government faced what was,
excepting the Civil War, its greatest test. [6] As Hopkins
pointed out:

> To have let things take their course—in accordance
> with precedent—would have meant taking a major
> step toward the destruction of the American system.
> It would have meant such a concentration of feudal
> overlordship at the top and economic serfdom at
> the bottom that the American way would have be-
> come a mere memory. [7]

In short, the consequences of continued federal inaction,
many observers felt, either would have been revolution and
the demise of democracy supplanted by some form of
dictatorship or a deliberate repression of the people, with
return toward some of the inequities of the Middle
Ages. [8]

However, Roosevelt seized upon another option: a program of recovery and reform that would bind the nation
together—this time not geographically, but socially and
economically, nationwide. This would prove to be another
kind of "revolution," peacefully effected, within the
bounds of federalism and in the context of democracy.

This form of constitutional revolution was the genius of Roosevelt and, to a marked degree, the handiwork of Harry Hopkins.

Hopkins' Contribution

Basil Rauch has noted that there were two New Deals, and that the recovery instituted by the First New Deal led to the reform instituted by the Second. [9] In retrospect, it becomes clear that Hopkins played a pivotal role in shaping and executing both the recovery and the reform of the 1930s, and, with Roosevelt, was principal architect and builder of a modern social welfare administration.

Although many people have viewed Roosevelt as the builder, available evidence does not confirm this simplistic assignment of functions. Hopkins appears to have been a principal architect in his own right, designing much of the plan for recovery and many of the subsequent reforms. He was not a mere engineer or technician. The remarkable fact that emerges from a study of Hopkins' work during the 1930s is that he had the creativity and administrative competence to play both roles: that of planner, designer or architect, on the one hand, and that of administrator, contractor or builder on the other. That the President and the Congress gave Hopkins such a decisive role in shaping social policy is, in part, a tribute to their confidence in him. This confidence would appear to have come in large measure from their knowledge of his capacity to execute an efficient program once policy was established. Hence, Hopkins' ability as architect gave him the right framework within which to build; and, similarly, his capacity as an administrator afforded him the freedom and political support to frame new policy decisions.

The Impact of Recovery

Recovery was both a psychology and a program. The nation
was at a low point in modern history, not merely because
the economic situation was so bad, but because the mood
of the people held little hope of conditions getting better.
There was a prevailing despair among the millions of unemployed based upon their feeling that the government was
not listening, that the leaders were not leading, and that the
democratic system was not working. For some, there was
simply a feeling of hopelessness and helplessness; among
others, there was resentment and anger. Whether revolution
would have taken place if Hoover had been reelected and
maintained his policies never will be known. It would have
depended, in part, on how much of the passivity from
hunger turned into aggression from fear.

Hopkins understood the fear in the country just as did
Roosevelt, and the first and major task of the recovery
effort was the restoration of hope and renewal of confidence in the responsiveness of the democratic system.
More than anything else, the speed with which Hopkins
got the FERA underway and the funds out to the states
and to the people was a symbol that somebody in Washington understood, somebody cared. This new feeling for
people as the primary resource to be nourished and con-
served was in marked contrast to the policies of the Hoover
Administration, where the interests of business were put
ahead of the needs of unemployed people. Hoover's interest
in fiscal factors was not merely economic, but was mirrored
in social welfare programs as well, where economy and
efficiency were the primary values in administration. Hopkins believed that, while these values were not to be
scorned, a more positive approach was needed which would
underscore delivery of services to the people. In rejecting the emphasis on audit and control, Hopkins said

that the *individual* "must be the first and last digit in all government accounting." [10]

The second aspect of recovery involved building a sound program. During this earlier period (1933-1935), Hopkins employed new structures using old methods. The FERA was the new structure and the grant-in-aid mechanism was the tried and tested tool for disbursement. Because of his emphasis on the need for speed, he had no faith in what he called the "trickle-down theory" of Ickes' PWA. The people needed jobs and money immediately if psychological and economic recovery were to take place. Therefore, Hopkins believed in a "trickle-up theory": put money in the hands of the poor and it will soak upward and nourish the whole economic structure. [11] Perhaps no decision which Hopkins made in these early years was as important as this one, for it speeded the process of economic recovery, on the one hand, while addressing the psychological needs of the people, on the other.

Were the emergency programs of the recovery successful? This question can be answered best by the outcome, the results. As we have seen, the threat to democracy had been very great during the close of the Hoover Administration and continued to mount as Roosevelt came into office. Lorena Hickok, Hopkins' faithful "eyes and ears" as Chief Field Investigator, noticed Communist activity all over the country. "They are very busy," she wrote from Aberdeen, South Dakota, "getting right down among the farmers and working like beavers." The unemployed in Pennsylvania, she felt, were "right on the edge.... It wouldn't take much to make Communists out of them," she added. [12]

It is a matter of record that confidence in democracy was restored and that America weathered this crucial period when good men were considering an alternative system. This was the achievement of the First New Deal, when emergency measures were called forth to meet the challenge.

Now, in the Second New Deal, Hopkins would begin to carve out permanent programs of reform for a nation that had begun to recover.

The Impact of Reform

Despite a youthful flirtation with socialism, Hopkins was committed to the capitalistic system; but, if that system were to survive, he argued, it would have to change. What Hopkins had in mind were adaptations that capitalism, like any other system, would have to make in order to survive changing conditions. If this meant that certain permanent government programs had to be grafted onto the structure of capitalism to promote employment and ensure security, then this should be done. It was far more important to choose an adaptive model, Hopkins would argue, than to take the risks involved in maintaining a rigidity under changing conditions. *Time* magazine remarked that Hopkins was convinced "that the way to make the capitalistic system strong was to give it a socialistic appendix. . . . " [13]

Hence, the key to reform became the adaptive model, and its application was everywhere throughout New Deal social programs. The constitutionality of such measures lay in the later decision delivered by Supreme Court Justice Benjamin Cardozo in 1937:

> ... Congress may spend money in aid of the general welfare.... Nor is the concept of the general welfare static. Needs that were narrow or parochial a century ago may be interwoven in our day with the well-being of a nation. What is critical or urgent changes with the times. [14]

With this support for a flexible construction of the "general welfare clause" of the Constitution, the U.S. Supreme Court opened the doors for institutionalization of the First New Deal into broad programs of reform which would characterize the Second.

The nature of the reforms must be understood apart from the reforms themselves. By this, we mean that the impact of reform was greater than the sum of the reforms, for a philosophy was being implemented as well. Roosevelt and Hopkins were determined that the essence of reform was going to involve taking the control of government away from the corporate and financial structure and returning it to its rightful place in the hands of elected officials. Implied, of course, was a departure from the concept of laissez-faire in favor of having the initiative and control stem from government. In this manner, Roosevelt and Hopkins, with deliberate planning, took control of the American economy away from Wall Street and brought it to the seat of government in Washington.

Not only did this decision precipitate an overall enlargement of the federal government but also a change in the role which it would assume. Implicit in the nature of Roosevelt's and Hopkins' plan was an affirmation of the federal government's new and primary responsibility for social welfare functions. Moreover, not only would the government be perceived henceforth as a social instrument, but also, social welfare functions now should be adjudged a just claim on the public purse. In this sense, Roosevelt and Hopkins were architects of a fundamental change in the role and function of government in the United States.

Hopkins and Reform

There were four major reforms involving social welfare administration during the Second New Deal, and Harry Hopkins played a major role in every one.

First, Hopkins was perhaps the central figure in persuading Roosevelt to adopt an economic policy of deficit-spending. Without this principle of budgeting it would not have been possible to institute the broad spectrum of social programs that characterized the mid- and late-1930s.

Second, Hopkins revolutionized the field of intergovernmental relations in 1935 by developing the WPA as an ongoing, direct federal program. This decision marked one of the earliest recognitions of the growing urbanization in America and thus the need to develop federal-municipal relations. That Hopkins could do this in an acceptable and effective manner served, in large measure, to usher in a new era in intergovernmental relations and to kindle a spirit of cooperative federalism.

Third, Hopkins made a major contribution toward design of the first program of social insurance in America. As a member of the five-man Committee on Economic Security, Hopkins must be credited not only with shaping the recommendations which became the 1935 Social Security Act, but also must be recognized for his advocacy of health insurance, coverage for children with unemployed fathers, and inclusion of domestic and agricultural workers—all of which have been enacted in subsequent amendments to the original legislation.

Fourth, Hopkins designed the first large-scale program of public work in this country—the WPA. The Works Progress Administration was revolutionary in concept not only because it implied a permanent responsibility of government for the unemployed—which it did—but also because it brought social work and social welfare administration once and for all into the public arena. In short, the federal government was saying for the first time that it recognized its accountability for relief; and, furthermore, that administration of public social services henceforth would be a professional responsibility.

Hopkins' Imprint

We know that something remarkable happened in social welfare during the 1930s. Many variables are involved in an explanation of why events took place as they did, and the complexity of the subject defies a facile interpretation. What now becomes evident, however, is that a major factor in the change process was a man—Harry Hopkins—who largely has been ignored by historians, political scientists and social welfare practitioners. There is compelling evidence to document his impact on the plans and programs of this decade, and his imprint on the evolution of a modern program of public welfare administration in America.

In seven years of state and federal service, Hopkins played a pivotal role in this nation's most impressive program of recovery and its most far-reaching schema of reform. In the first instance, he helped to restore life to the American system of governing through rebuilding the minds and bodies of people, and, at the same time, remodeling an archaic social welfare system. In the second instance, Hopkins took aggressive leadership in forging new precedents and permanent new programs which would alter social welfare administration more in one decade than in the previous century and a half.

The 1930s were a crucial decade for social welfare administration because it marked the founding of our present system of modern public welfare. In great measure, Harry Hopkins was responsible for this "revolutionary evolution"—from poor law to public welfare—and his contribution has made an indelible imprint on our current way of life. Harry L. Hopkins has bequeathed a priceless legacy to the American people.

1. Harry L. Hopkins, *What Is the "American Way"?* (Washington: Works Progress Administration, 1938), p. 4. Only a month after Roosevelt had been elected President, Hopkins wrote his brother, "It seems to me that the principal idea of the public administrators for the past several years has been to protect big business, and I have a great deal more confidence in the 'hoi polloi' that are going into office on the fourth of March than I ever had in Andy Mellon and his crowd of highbinders. . . . " Ellis, *A Nation in Torment*, p. 490.

2. Gifford Pinchot, "The Case for Federal Relief," *Survey*, LXVII (January 1, 1932) , p. 348.

3. David Shannon, ed., *The Great Depression* (Englewood Cliffs, N.J.: Prentice-Hall Co., 1960), p. 111. For a full discussion of the possibility of an uprising in 1932-33, see Ch. VII: "Will There Be a Revolution?"

4. Bernstein, *Lean Years*, pp. 466-67.

5. Ernest K. Lindley, *The Roosevelt Revolution* (New York: The Viking Press, 1933), p. 14.

6. Arthur M. Schlesinger, Jr., *Crisis of the Old Order, 1919-1933* (Boston: Houghton-Mifflin Co., 1957), p. 484.

7. Hopkins, *What Is the "American Way"?*, pp. 5-6.

8. See Paul A. Kurzman, "Poor Relief in Medieval England: The Forgotten Chapter in the History of Social Welfare," *Child Welfare* (November 1970), pp. 495-501.

9. See Basil Rauch, *The History of the New Deal* (New York: Creative Age Press, 1944).

10. Hopkins, *Spending to Save*, p. 178.

11. Phillips, *Crash to Blitz*, p. 267.

12. Letter, Lorena Hickok to Harry Hopkins, November 7, 1933; Report on Pennsylvania, Hickok to Hopkins, Week of August 7-12, 1933, Hickok File, Hopkins MSS, Hyde Park Collection.

13. "Men at Work," *Time*, July 18, 1938, p. 9.

14. Guy T. Helvering et al. *v.* George P. Davis, 301 U.S. 619 (May 24, 1937).

Bibliography

Books

Abbott, Grace. *From Relief to Social Security: The Development of the New Public Welfare Services and Their Administration.* Chicago: University of Chicago Press, 1941.

Adams, Grace K. *Workers on Relief.* New Haven, Conn.: Yale University Press, 1939.

Alsberg, Henry G. *America Fights the Depression.* New York: Coward-McCann, 1934.

Alsop, Joseph and Kintner, Robert. *Men Around the President.* New York: Doubleday, Doran and Co., 1939.

Altmeyer, Arthur J. *The Formative Years of Social Security.* Madison: University of Wisconsin Press, 1966.

American Association of Social Workers. *This Business of Relief.* New York: Privately Published, 1936.

Anderson, Nels. *The Right to Work.* New York: Modern Age Books, 1938.

Anderson, Patrick. *The Presidents' Men.* Garden City, N.Y.: Doubleday and Co., 1968.

Asbell, Bernard. *The F.D.R. Memoirs.* New York: Doubleday and Co., 1973.

Bakke, E. Wight. *The Unemployed Worker.* New Haven, Conn.: Yale University Press, 1940.

Bellush, Bernard. *Franklin D. Roosevelt as Governor of New York.* New York: Columbia University Press, 1955.

Bernstein, Irving. *The Lean Years.* Boston: Houghton Mifflin, 1960.

Betters, Paul V. *Federal Services to Municipal Governments.* Washington: The Brookings Institution, 1931.

_____. Williams, J. Kerwin; and Reeder, Sherwood L. *Recent Federal-City Relations.* Washington: U.S. Conference of Mayors, 1936.

Blum, John M. *From the Morgenthau Diaries: Years of Crises, 1928-1938.* Boston: Houghton Mifflin Co., 1959.

Breckinridge, Sophonisba P. *Public Welfare Administration in the United States.* Chicago: University of Chicago Press, 1938.

Brown, Josephine C. *Public Relief, 1929-1939.* New York: Henry Holt and Co., 1940.

Brown, Pamela. *Analysis of Civil Works Program Statistics.* Washington: Works Progress Administration, 1939.

Brownlow, Louis. *A Passion for Anonymity: The Autobiography of Louis Brownlow.* Chicago: University of Chicago Press, 1958.

Bruno, Frank J. *Trends in Social Work: 1874-1956.* New York: Columbia University Press, 1957.

Burns, Arthur E. and Williams, Edward A. *Federal Work, Security and Relief Programs.* Washington: U.S. Government Printing Office, 1941.

Burns, Eveline M. *The American Social Security System.* Boston: Houghton Mifflin Co., 1949.

Burns, James M. *Roosevelt: The Lion and the Fox.* New York: Harcourt, Brace and Co., 1956.

Carothers, Doris. *Chronology of the Federal Emergency Relief Administration.* Research Monograph VI. Washington: U.S. Government Printing Office, 1937.

[Carter, John Franklin.] *The New Dealers.* New York: Simon and Schuster, 1934.

Chandler, Lester V. *America's Greatest Depression, 1929-1941.* New York: Harper and Row, 1970.

Chapin, F. Stuart and Queen, Stuart A. *Social Work in the Depression.* Bulletin No. 39. New York: Social Science Research Council, 1937.

Charles, Searle F. *Minister of Relief: Harry Hopkins and the Depression.* Syracuse, N.Y.: Syracuse University Press, 1963.

Colcord, Joanna C. *Cash Relief.* New York: Russell Sage Foundation, 1936.

_____. Kaplovitz, William C.; and Kurtz, Russell H. *Emergency Work Relief.* New York: Russell Sage Foundation, 1932.

Conkin, Paul K. *F.D.R. and the Origins of the Welfare State.* New York: Thomas Y. Crowell Co., 1967.

Degler, Carl N., ed. *The New Deal*. Chicago: Quadrangle Books, 1970.

Dewey, Thomas E. *The Case Against the New Deal*. New York: Harper and Brothers, 1940.

Eccles, Marriner S. *Beckoning Frontiers*. edited by Sidney Hyman. New York: Alfred A. Knopf Inc., 1951.

Ekirch, Arthur A., Jr. *Ideologies and Utopias: The Impact of the New Deal on American Thought*. Chicago: Quadrangle Books, 1969.

Ellis, Edward Robb. *A Nation in Torment: The Great Depression, 1929-1939*. New York: Coward-McCann, 1970.

Enzler, Clarence J. *Some Social Aspects of the Depression*. Washington: Catholic University of America Press, 1939.

Feder, Leah Hannah. *Unemployment Relief in Periods of Depression*. New York: Russell Sage Foundation, 1936.

Flynn, John T. *The Roosevelt Myth*. rev. ed., New York: Devin-Adair Co., 1956.

Freidel, Frank. *The New Deal and the American People*. Englewood Cliffs, N.J.: Prentice-Hall, 1964.

Fusfield, Daniel R. *The Economic Thought of Franklin D. Roosevelt*. New York: Columbia University Press, 1956.

Gill, Corrington. *Wasted Manpower*. New York: W.W. Norton Co., 1939.

Hayes, E.P. *Activities of the President's Emergency Committee for Employment*. Concord, N.H.: The Rumford Press, 1936.

High, Stanley. *Roosevelt—and Then?* New York: Harper and Brothers, 1937.

Hofstadter, Richard. *The Age of Reform*. New York: Alfred A. Knopf, 1955.

Hoover, Herbert. *The Great Depression, 1929-1941*. New York: The Macmillan Co., 1952, Vol. III.

Hopkins, Harry L. *Principal Speeches of Harry L. Hopkins*. Milwaukee, Wisc., no publisher named, 1938.

_____. *Spending to Save: The Complete Story of Relief*. New York: W.W. Norton and Co., 1936.

_____. *The Realities of Unemployment*. Washington: Work Projects Administration, 1937.

_____. *What Is the "American Way"?* Washington: Works Progress Administration, 1938.

Howard, Donald S. *The WPA and Federal Relief Policy*. New York: Russell Sage Foundation, 1943.

Ickes, Harold L. *Back to Work: The Story of the PWA*. New York: The Macmillan Co., 1935.

_____ . *The Secret Diary of Harold L. Ickes.* New York: Simon and Schuster, 1953.

Johnson, Hugh S. *The Blue Eagle: From Egg to Earth.* Garden City, N.Y.: Doubleday, Doran and Co., 1935.

Joslin, Theodore G. *Hoover Off the Record.* Garden City, N.Y.: Doubleday, Doran and Co., 1935.

Karl, Barry D. *Executive Reorganization and Reform in the New Deal.* Cambridge, Mass.: Harvard University Press, 1963.

Key, V.O., Jr. *The Administration of Federal Grants to States.* Chicago: Public Administration Service, 1937.

Koenig, Louis W. *The Invisible Presidency.* New York: Rinehart and Co., Inc., 1960.

Laidler, Harry W. *Program for Modern America.* New York: Thomas Y. Crowell Co., 1936.

Lane, Marie Dresden and Steegmuller, Francis. *America on Relief.* New York: Harcourt, Brace and Co., 1938.

Leuchtenburg, William E. *Franklin D. Roosevelt and the New Deal, 1932-1940.* New York: Harper and Row, 1963.

_____ . ed. *The New Deal: A Documentary History.* Columbia, S.C.: University of South Carolina Press, 1968.

Lindley, Ernest K. *The Roosevelt Revolution.* New York: The Viking Press, 1933.

Macdonald, Austin F. *Federal Aid.* New York: Thomas Y. Crowell Co., 1928.

Macmahon, A.W.; Millett, J.D.; and Ogden, Gladys. *The Administration of Federal Work Relief.* Chicago: Public Administration Service, 1941.

Malthus, Thomas R. *An Essay on the Principle of Population.* Homewood, Ill.: R.D. Irwin, 1963.

Mangione, Jerre G. *The Dream and the Deal: The Federal Writers' Project, 1935-1943.* Boston: Little, Brown Co., 1972.

Meriam, Lewis. *Relief and Social Security.* Washington: The Brookings Institution, 1946.

Mitchell, Broadus. *The Depression Decade.* New York: Rinehart and Co., 1947.

Moley, Raymond. *After Seven Years.* New York: Harper and Brothers, 1939.

_____ . *The First New Deal.* New York: Harcourt, Brace and World, 1966.

Myers, W. S. and Newton, W. H. *The Hoover Administration: A Documented Narrative.* New York: Charles Scribner's Sons, 1936.

Perkins, Frances. *The Roosevelt I Knew.* New York: Viking Press, 1946.

Phillips, Cabell. *From the Crash to the Blitz: 1929-1939.* New York: The Macmillan Co., 1969.

Radomski, Alexander L. *Work Relief in New York State: 1931-1935.* New York: King's Crown Press, 1947.

Rauch, Basil. *The History of the New Deal.* New York: Creative Age Press, 1944.

Richberg, Donald R. *My Hero.* New York: G. P. Putnam's Sons, 1954.

Richmond, Mary. *What Is Social Case Work?.* New York: Russell Sage Foundation, 1922.

Robinson, Virginia P. *A Changing Psychology in Social Case Work.* Chapel Hill, N. C.: University of North Carolina Press, 1930.

Roosevelt, Eleanor. *This I Remember.* New York: Harper and Brothers, 1949.

Rosenman, Samuel I., ed. *The Public Papers and Addresses of Franklin D. Roosevelt.* New York: Random House; Macmillan, 1938-1950.

——————— . *Working with Roosevelt.* New York: Harper and Brothers, 1952.

Sanders, Daniel S. *The Impact of Reform Movements on Social Policy Change: The Case of Social Insurance.* Fair Lawn, N.J.: R. E. Burdick, Inc., 1973.

Schlesinger, Arthur M., Jr. *The Coming of the New Deal.* Boston: Houghton Mifflin Co., 1958.

——————— . *The Politics of Upheaval,* Boston: Houghton Mifflin Co., 1960.

Shannon, David, ed. *The Great Depression.* Englewood Cliffs, N. J.: Prentice-Hall Co., 1960.

Sherwood, Robert E. *Roosevelt and Hopkins: An Intimate History.* rev. ed., New York: Harper and Brothers, 1950.

Stevenson, Marietta. *Public Welfare Administration.* New York: The Macmillan Co., 1938.

Tugwell, Rexford G. *The Democratic Roosevelt,* Garden City, N. Y.: Doubleday and Co., 1957.

——————— . *F.D.R., Architect of an Era.* New York: Macmillan Co., 1967.

——————— . *The Brains Trust.* New York: Viking Press, 1968.

Tully, Grace. *F.D.R., My Boss.* New York: Charles Scribner's Sons, 1949.

Waldo, Dwight. *The Study of Public Administration.* New York:

Random House, 1955.

Wecter, Dixon. *Age of the Great Depression.* New York: Macmillan Co., 1948.

Weissman, Irving, ed. *Social Work Curriculum Study.* New York: Council on Social Work Education, 1959. Vols. 3, 7 and 12.

Wilbur, R.L. and Hyde, A.M. *The Hoover Policies.* New York: Charles Scribner's Sons, 1937.

Wilensky, Harold L. and Lebeaux, Charles N. *Industrial Society and Social Welfare.* New York: Russell Sage Foundation, 1958.

Williams, Edward A. *Federal Aid for Relief.* New York: Columbia University Press, 1939.

——————————. *Work, Relief and Security.* Washington: U.S. Government Printing Office, 1941.

Witte, Edwin. *Development of the Social Security Act.* Madison, Wisc.: University of Wisconsin Press, 1962.

Wolters, Raymond. *Negroes and the Great Depression.* Westport, Conn.: Greenwood Publishing Co., 1970.

Woodroofe, Kathleen. *From Charity to Social Work.* Toronto: University of Toronto Press, 1966.

Zinn, Howard, ed. *New Deal Thought.* Indianapolis, Ind.: Bobbs-Merrill Co., 1966.

Reference Works

Hall, Fred S., ed. *Social Work Year Book.* New York: Russell Sage Foundation, 1929, 1933, 1935.

Hamer, Philip M., ed. *Guide to Archives and Manuscripts in the United States.* New Haven, Conn.: Yale University Press, 1961.

Kurtz, Russell H., ed. *Social Work Year Book.* New York: Russell Sage Foundation, 1937, 1939.

Library of Congress. *National Union Catalogue of Manuscript Collections.* Washington, D.C.: Library of Congress, 1959.

Morris, Robert, ed.-in-chief; Saunders, Beatrice, staff ed.-in-chief. *Encyclopedia of Social Work.* New York: National Association of Social Workers, 1971.

Powell, C. Percy, ed. *List of Manuscript Collections in the Library of Congress, July 1931 to July 1938.* Washington, D.C.: Library of Congress, 1939.

Seligman, Edwin, ed. *Encyclopedia of the Social Sciences,* 1st edition. New York: Macmillan, 1931.

Articles

Abbott, Edith. "Pauper Laws Still Go On." *Social Service Review,* IX (December 1935), pp. 731-56.
──────────. "Don't Do It, Mr. Hopkins!" *Nation,* January 9, 1935, pp. 41-42.
Bane, Frank. "Public Welfare in 1934." *Social Service Review,* VIII (September 1934), pp. 408-14.
Belair, Felix. "Harry L. Hopkins: Lender and Spender." *Life Magazine,* September 22, 1941, pp. 88-99.
Benjamin, Paul L. "Unemployment and Relief." *The Family,* XVI (May 1935), pp. 67-71.
Childs, Marquis. "The President's Best Friend," *Saturday Evening Post,* April 19 & 26, 1941, pp. 9-11ff and 29ff.
Clapper, Raymond. "Who Is Hopkins?" *Forum,* XCVIII (December 1937), pp. 283-87.
The Compass, IV (March 1934), pp. 1-27.
Creel, George. "One-Round Hopkins." *Collier's,* November 9, 1935, pp. 37ff.
Hamilton, Gordon. "Case Work Responsibility in the Unemployment Relief Agency." *The Family,* XV (July 1934), pp. 135-41.
"Harry Hopkins." *Fortune Magazine,* XII (July 1935), pp. 58-64ff.
Hellman, Geoffrey T. "Profile of Harry Hopkins." *The New Yorker.* August 7 & 14, 1943, pp. 25-28ff & 27-30ff.
Hopkins, Harry L. "The Gigantic Task of Winter Relief." *New York Times,* September 24, 1933.
──────────. "Federal Relief Job." *Survey,* LXIX (July 1933), pp. 247ff.
──────────. "The Developing National Program of Relief." *Proceedings of the National Conference of Social Work* (Chicago: University of Chicago Press, 1933).
──────────. "A Statement to the Relief Legislators by the Federal Relief Administration." *State Government,* VI (September 1933), pp. 8-10.
──────────. "The War on Distress." *Today,* December 16, 1933, pp. 8-9ff.
──────────. "The F.E.R.A. and the Recovery Program." *Dun and Bradstreet Monthly Review,* XLII (April 1934), pp. 2-4.
──────────. "Giving 16 Million People a New Chance." *Today,* June 30, 1934, pp. 6-7.
──────────. "Beyond Relief: The Larger Task," *New York*

Times (Magazine Section), August 19, 1934.

—————————. "Social Planning for the Future." *Social Service Review,* VIII (September 1934), pp. 397-407.

—————————. "How Will They Get Through the Winter?" (with Henry F. Pringle) *The American Magazine,* December 1934.

—————————. "17,000,000 on Government Relief Despite Returning Prosperity." *Washington Herald,* January 6, 1935.

—————————. "Hope for the Millions." *Today,* May 4, 1935, pp. 3-4ff.

—————————. "Supplementing the Dole with Jobs." *United States News,* May 13, 1935.

—————————. "How Can the States Help?" *State Government,* VIII (September 1935).

—————————. "They'd Rather Work." *Collier's,* November 16, 1935, pp. 7-9ff.

—————————. "Food for the Hungry." *Collier's,* December 7, 1935, pp. 10-11ff.

—————————. "Boondoggling: It Is a Social Asset." *Christian Science Monitor* (Magazine Section), August 19, 1936.

—————————. "The Future of Relief." *New Republic,* February 10, 1937, pp. 7-10.

—————————. "The WPA Looks Forward." *Survey Midmonthly,* LXXIV (June 1938), pp. 195-98.

Huzar, Elias. "Federal Unemployment Relief Policies." *Journal of Politics,* II (June 1940), pp. 321-35.

Kluckhohn, Frank. "Hopkins Confident as a Goal Is Reached." *New York Times* (Magazine Section), December 8, 1935.

Lundberg, Emma O. "The New York State Temporary Emergency Relief Administration." *Social Service Review,* VI (December 1932), pp. 545-66.

Lurie, Harry L. "The Place of Federal Aid in Unemployment Relief." *Social Service Review,* V (December 1931) pp. 523-38.

Mitchell, Jonathan. "Alms-Giver: Harry L. Hopkins." *New Republic,* April 10, 1935, pp. 235-38.

Perkins, Frances. "People Mattered to Harry Hopkins." *Survey Midmonthly,* LXXXII (February 1946), pp. 38-39.

Pinchot, Gifford. "The Case for Federal Relief." *Survey,* LXVII (January 1, 1932), pp. 347-49ff.

"Relief: Men at Work." *Time,* July 18, 1938, pp. 9-11.

"Relief: Professional Giver." *Time,* February 19, 1934, pp. 11-13.

Sherwood, Robert E. "The Secret Papers of Harry L. Hopkins:

He Wanted to Be President." *Colliers,* May 29, 1948.

Springer, Gertrude. "The New Deal and the Old Dole." *Survey Graphic,* XXII (July 1933), pp. 347-52ff.

Stark, Lewis. "Work Relief Corporation to Spend 8 to 9 Billions— Hopkins to End Dole." *New York Times,* December 2, 1934, Section IV.

Sugrue, Thomas. "Hopkins Holds the Bag." *The American Magazine,* March 1936, pp. 27; 149-53.

Wallerstein, Helen. "New Trends in Case Work as Developed by the Depression." *The Family,* XV (November 1934), pp. 206-10.

Ward, Paul W. "Dirge for Mr. Hopkins." *Nation,* May 22, 1935, pp. 594-96.

Williams, Edward A. and Williams, J. Kerwin. "The WPA Method vs. Grants-in-Aid." *Survey Midmonthly,* LXXVI (March 1940), pp. 91-93.

Wolfe, Bertram D. "The Case of Harry L. Hopkins." *American Mercury,* LXVIII (January 1949), pp. 109-116.

Reports and Unpublished Material

American Association of Social Workers. "A Survey of the Current Relief Situation in 43 Representative Areas in 28 States of the United States: Winter of 1938." (mimeographed), March 21, 1938.

American Public Welfare Association. *Proceedings of National Conference.* (1931-1936), Washington, D.C.

Congressional Record. 73d—75th Congress. (1932-1938). Washington, U.S. Government Printing Office.

Cotham, Perry C. "Harry L. Hopkins: Spokesman for Franklin D. Roosevelt in Depression and War." Unpublished Ph.D. Dissertation, Wayne State University, 1970.

Hartman, Ann. "Casework in Crisis: 1932-1941." Unpublished D.S.W. Dissertation, Columbia University, 1972.

Hellenbrand, Shirley C. "Main Currents in Social Casework: 1918-1936." Unpublished D.S.W. Dissertation, Columbia University, 1965.

National Conference of Social Work. *Proceedings of Annual Meetings. (1929-1938),* Chicago, University of Chicago Press.

National Emergency Council. *Activities of the Federal Emergency Agencies, 1933-1938.* Report No. 7. October, 1938.

National Resources Planning Board. *National Resources Development: Report for 1942.* Washington: U.S. Government Printing Office, 1942.

Social Science Research Council. *Social Aspects of Research Policies.* Bulletin No. 38, edited by R.C. White and M.K. White. New York. 1937.

Spector, Stephen. "Harry L. Hopkins, 1890-1933." Unpublished M.A. Thesis, New York University, February 1964.

Temporary Emergency Relief Administration. *Five Million People—One Billion Dollars.* Final Report of the New York State T.E.R.A. (November 1, 1931-June 30, 1937), Albany, N.Y., 1937.

_____ . *Three Years of Public Unemployment Relief in New York State.* Interim Report of the New York State T.E.R.A., Albany, N.Y., 1934.

Work Projects Administration. *Chronology of Federal Relief Legislation, 1932-1939.* Prepared by the Legislative Reference Service, U.S. Federal Works Agency, December 1939, revised.

_____ . *Final Statistical Report of the Federal Emergency Relief Administration.* edited by T.E. Whiting, Washington, 1941.

Interviews by Author

Bane, Frank. April 21, 1970.
Burns, Eveline M. May 11, 1970.
Gulick, Luther. December 4, 1969.
Koenig, Louis W. April 16, 1970.
Moley, Raymond. March 26, 1970.
Rosenman, Samuel I. April 1, 1970.

Manuscript Collections

Franklin D. Roosevelt Library. (Hyde Park, New York)
Oral History Research Office, Columbia University. (New York, New York)
Library of Congress, Manuscript Division. (Washington, D. C.)
National Archives, Social and Economic Records Division. (Washington, D. C.)

Index of Names

Index of Names

Mitchell, Jonathan, 186, 191n, 212.
Moley, Raymond, 32, 88, 91n, 135, 140, 142n, 143n, 156, 160n, 208, 214.
Morgenthau, Henry, 38, 133.
Morris, Robert, 210.
Moynihan, Patrick, 22.
Myers, William S., 66n, 208.

Nathan, Robert R., 65n.
Newton, Isaac, 62.
Newton, Walter H., 66n, 208.
Nixon, Richard M., 22-24.

Ogden, Gladys, 99n, 116n, 117n, 142n, 143n, 180, 191n, 208.

Perkins, Frances R., 31, 32, 125, 141n, 148, 151n, 183, 191n, 209, 212.
Phillips, Cabell, 41n, 115, 117n, 118n, 143n, 160n, 203n, 209.
Pierce, Franklin, 49, 52, 89.
Pinchot, Gifford, 203n, 212.
Post, Robert P., 91n.
Powell, C. Percy, 210.
Pyle, Ernie, 153, 154, 160n.

Queen, Stuart A., 206.

Radomski, Alexander L., 75n, 209.
Rasputin, Grigori, 155, 160n.
Rauch, Basil, 196, 203n, 209.
Reeder, Sherwood L., 117n, 141n, 190, 192n, 206.
Richberg, Donald, 147, 151n, 209.
Richmond, Mary, 48, 166, 176n, 209.

Robinson, Virginia, 166, 177n, 209.
Roosevelt, Eleanor, 209.
Roosevelt, Franklin D., 10, 13-17, 21, 28, 29, 31, 32, 38, 39, 62, 64, 65n, 67, 69-74, 75n, 76n, 77, 79, 81, 87, 91n, 93, 95-97, 102-104, 106, 111-115, 118n, 119, 122, 124, 126, 132, 133, 135-137, 139, 140, 145-150, 159, 165, 178n, 183, 188, 193, 195-198, 200, 201, 203n.
Roosevelt, Theodore, 147.
Rosenheim, Margaret K., 141n.
Rosenman, Samuel I., 32, 87, 89n, 90n, 91n, 98, 99n, 139, 140, 143n, 145, 151n, 209, 214.

Sanders, Daniel S., 141n, 209.
Saunders, Beatrice, 210.
Schlesinger, Arthur, Jr., 137, 141n, 142n, 160n, 195, 203n, 209.
Seligman, Edwin, 53n, 210.
Shannon, David, 194, 203n, 209.
Sherwood, Robert E., 28, 38, 41n, 74n, 115n, 139, 143n, 151n, 160n, 191n, 209, 212.
Shriver, Paul D., 191n.
Spector, Stephen, 214.
Springer, Gertrude, 213.
Stalin, Joseph, 38.
Stark, Lewis, 213.
Steegmuller, Francis, 208.
Stevenson, Marietta, 209.
Stokes, Thomas L., 139, 143n.
Straus, Jesse I., 71, 72, 75n.
Straus, Robert K., 32.
Strong, Silas, 57.

Sugrue, Thomas, 213.
Sullivan, John, 71.
Sytz, Florence, 187, 192n.

Taft, William Howard, 16, 17.
Truman, Harry S., 67.
Tugwell, Rexford, 31, 32, 96, 99n, 149, 151n, 156, 209.
Tully, Grace, 151n, 209.
Tzu, Lao, 37.

Urwick, Lyndall, 25, 190, 192n.

van Waters, Miriam, 164, 176n.

Wagner, Robert F., Sr., 64n.
Waldo, Dwight, 191n, 209.
Walker, Frank, 116n.
Wallace, Henry, 31.
Wallerstein, Helen, 213.
Ward, Paul W., 213.
Webb, Beatrice and Sidney, 125.
Wecter, Dixon, 89n, 118n, 210.
Weissman, Irving, 192n, 210.
Westbrook, Lawrence, 130.
Wickser, Philip, 71.
Wilbur, Ray L., 64n, 65n, 66n,

66n, 210.
Wilensky, Harold L., 210.
Wilkins, Roy, 194.
Williams, Aubrey, 32, 128, 130.
173, 175, 177n.
Williams, Edward A., 52n, 75n, 91n, 99n, 116n, 117n, 118n, 141n, 190, 192n, 206, 210, 213.
Williams, J. Kerwin, 116n, 117n, 206, 213.
Willkie, Wendell, 146.
Willoughby, William F., 191n.
Wilson, Woodrow, 147.
Wisner, Elizabeth, 32, 131, 142n, 171, 177n.
Witte, Edwin, 126, 127, 141n, 210.
Wolfe, Bertram D., 213.
Wolters, Raymond, 129, 142n, 210.
Woodroofe, Kathleen, 52n, 210.
Woods, Arthur, 57, 65n.
Woodward, Ellen, 130.
Wright, Helen, 53n.

Zinn, Howard, 117n, 142n, 210.

About the Author

PAUL A. KURZMAN is a social worker with a fondness for both program development and administration. He has served as Staff Director of the Two Bridges Neighborhood Council and as Acting Executive Director of the Lower Eastside Neighborhoods Association (LENA) in New York City. Most recently, he was Assistant Commissioner of the Youth Services Agency in New York's Human Resources Administration, and Director of the City's $30 million-a-year Neighborhood Youth Corps program.

Dr. Kurzman has served as a social welfare consultant in both the public and private sectors, has written extensively for professional journals, and is editor of a book on social welfare practice, *The Mississippi Experience: Strategies for Welfare Rights Action.*

He received an A.B. from Princeton, his Master's degree from the Columbia University School of Social Work, and a Ph.D. degree in public administration from New York University. Presently, Dr. Kurzman is Program Director of the Industrial Social Welfare Center of the Columbia University School of Social Work and Adjunct Assistant Professor, Hunter College School of Social Work, City University of New York.

About Louis W. Koenig

LOUIS W. KOENIG is a distinguished academician and respected observer of the American political process. Dr. Koenig gained personal experience serving in the Executive Branch during the 1940s with the First Hoover Commission and the U.S. Bureau of the Budget, and later, as a consultant to governmental organizations and foundations.

A prolific author of articles on contemporary political

systems, he also is the author of eight books on American governmental operations, including such classics as *Congress and the President* and *The Chief Executive*. Dr. Koenig is a nationally recognized authority on the executive branch of government, and on the formulation of public policy in a democratic society.

Professor Koenig received his M.A. and Ph.D. degrees from Columbia University, and was awarded an honorary doctorate at Bard College in 1960. Since 1950, he has been a member of the faculty of New York University, where he currently serves as Professor of Government.

THE TEXT for this book was composed by ESP, Inc., Nyack, New York 10960, using IBM Selectric Composer *Aldine Roman* type for text proper and Univers for running heads, folios, and Index.

THE LAKESIDE PRESS of the R.R. Donnelley & Sons Company printed this book on its Cameron Belt Press, provided the patent ("perfect") binding, and produced the jacket at its Crawfordsville, Indiana plant.